THE ISLE OF BUTE

THE ISLE OF BUTE

Norman Newton

David and Charles

CONTENTS

Half-title page: The Isle of Cumbrae preparing to leave Rhubodach on its five-minute journey across the Kyles to Colintraive

Title page: Fertile farmland on the raised beach above St Ninian's Bay

Left: The verdant interior of the Pavilion, Mount Stuart

INTRODUCING THE ISLAND

THE ISLAND OF BUTE lies in the Firth of Clyde, tucked in the shelter of the long, sinuous sea-lochs of the Argyll mainland, and dominated to the south by the high, rugged mountains of the island of Arran. It is within commuting distance of Glasgow and in its heyday was the destination for millions of Glaswegians escaping 'doon the watter' once a year from industrial drudgery, during the Glasgow Fair fortnight.

Bute is about 15 miles (24km) long and from 3–5 miles (5–8km) in width. To the north is the district of Cowal, part of Argyll, from which the island is separated by the scenically famous Kyles of Bute, a narrow sea passage. A ferry crosses this narrow strait from Colintraive (Gaelic, *caol an t's-naimh,* the strait of the swimming place) on the Cowal mainland to Rhubodach at the north end of Bute. Colintraive takes its name from the times when cattle were swum across the narrow 'kyle' or strait on their way to the markets of central Scotland. To the south-east of Bute are the islands of

Above: Colourful flower beds welcome summer travellers at Rothesay pier

Pages 6-7: The Kyles of Bute and the hills of Cowal from Balnakailly Bay

Left: Old Red Sandstone at Kerrycroy, with a glacial erratic perched on the shore

9

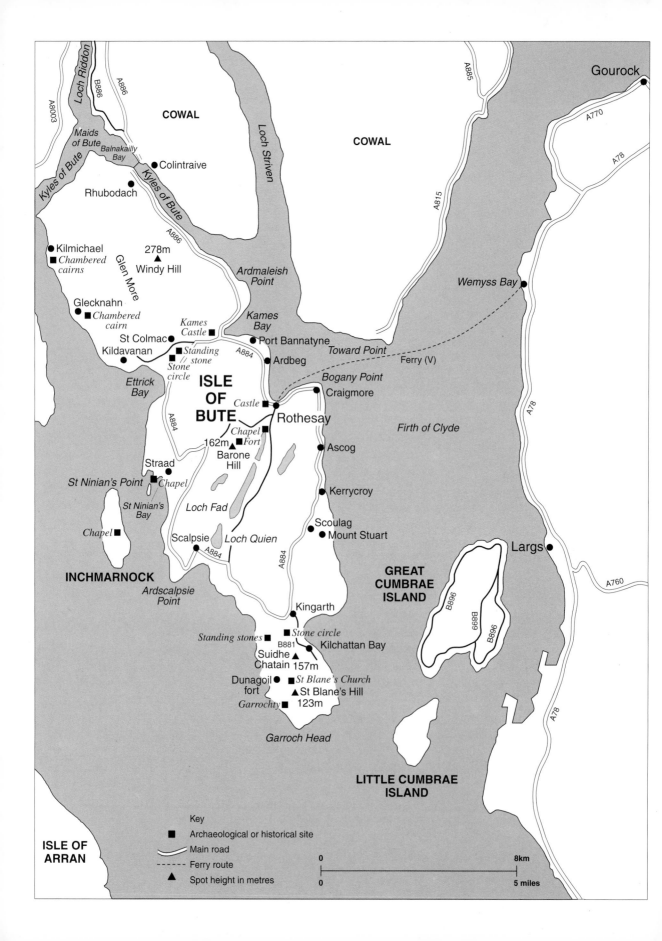

the Cumbraes, with the town of Largs and the Clyde coast tucked in behind.

Most visitors to Bute will arrive on the car ferry from Wemyss Bay (pronounced 'weems', from the Gaelic *uaim,* a cave) to Rothesay. Wemyss Bay is linked by train to Glasgow, so a day trip to Bute is eminently possible and there are even a handful of hardy commuters who travel from Rothesay to Glasgow daily. The ferry crossing takes about half an hour. The modern pier at Rothesay replaces an elegant Edwardian structure which burned down in 1962.

Geologically, Bute is interesting as it sits astride the Highland Boundary Fault, marked by Loch Fad, which almost cuts the island in two. To its north are Dalradian schists, to the south Old Red Sandstone and lava flows. Bute is a low-lying island, though in the northern end it is more hilly, rising to 912ft (278m) on Windy Hill. The climate of Bute is far drier and milder, and less windy, than most of Scotland's islands. Most of the rain that comes Bute's way falls on the high mountains of Arran, to the south-west.

The southern half of Bute is more low-lying and fertile, criss-crossed by roads, while the northern half of the island is wilder and rougher, with no roads at all away from the coastal fringe. The total land area of the island is 31,000 acres (12,555ha), divided into no fewer than eighty-four working farms, most of them rented from the principal landowner, the Marquess of Bute.

The ferry from Colintraive arriving at Rhubodach, at the north end of Bute

Overleaf: The mountains of Arran viewed from Dunagoil Bay, at the south end of Bute

Above: Palm trees grow well in Bute's mild climate, as here on the sea-front at Rothesay

Opposite: Farmland near Kingarth. The lowland areas of Bute are fertile and productive and agriculture is the mainstay of the island's economy

Calmac's 'streaker' car ferry Juno leaving Rothesay on its thirty-minute journey to Wemyss Bay on the Clyde coast. The Voith-Schneider propellers in the bow and stern allow great manoeuvrability

The resort of Rothesay, the main town and administrative centre on Bute, is one of the best known in Scotland, though now that it is competing with the air charter mass-tourist market this is not as true as it once was. The town is situated on the east coast of the island, facing Toward Point in Cowal and the Clyde coast.

With a population of 6,116 (1991 Census), Rothesay is very much the dominant settlement – the total population of Bute is only 7,354. Before the reorganisation of local government in 1975, 'Buteshire' included Arran and the Cumbraes, but now the island is lumped in with Argyll (and part of west Dunbartonshire) and administered from Lochgilphead by the Argyll and Bute Council – a rather clumsy arrangement.

Rothesay has shops of all kinds, banks, a post office, local authority offices, Rothesay Academy (the island's secondary school), a police station, hospital, health centre, swimming pool, public library and the Bute Museum, which is an essential stop for the interested visitor. The museum was built in 1926 by the 4th Marquess of Bute to house the archaeological and natural history collections in the care of the Buteshire Natural History Society. It was reorganised in 1950 and subsequently modernised and is an important example of a small, independent museum – rather old-fashioned, but full of interesting information and quality objects and artefacts.

Rothesay is well provided with hotels and guest-houses, from the refurbished 'hydropathic' Glenburn Hotel, with 137 rooms, to more humble but no less friendly bed and breakfast establishments.

Bute has some important attractions for visitors, notably the very early Rothesay Castle, the walls and gatehouse of which still survive, within a moat. It has had a long and fascinating history, involved in some of the key events of Scottish history. It was besieged by Norsemen in 1230, fell to King Haakon of Norway in 1263, and was captured from the English in 1334 at the end of the Wars of Independence. During the fifteenth century it was attacked by the Lord of the Isles. In 1544 the Earl of Lennox took it for the English. Cromwell installed a garrison during the civil wars of the seventeenth century; when this garrison was withdrawn in 1659 much of the castle buildings were dismantled and what remained was destroyed in the rebellions of 1685. After that, successive Marquesses of Bute began the process of restoration.

A more recent building, also rescued from decline and decay, is the Victorian Winter Garden, reopened in 1990 after a ten-year closure, at a cost of £850,000. This iron and glass building was once one of the most famous music halls in Scotland and is a welcome addition to Bute's leisure facilities. Its successful restoration is a tribute to what a small island community can accomplish, with assistance from a plethora of public agencies – testimony to the immense reservoir of goodwill which exists where islands are concerned.

St Mary's Chapel, in the High Street between the hospital and the creamery on the south edge of the town, dates from the thirteenth century and contains two medieval canopied wall tombs of a lady and a knight, possibly Robert II of Scotland or his father, Walter the Steward. The churchyard also contains the mausoleum of the Marquesses of Bute. The

THE DUKE OF ROTHESAY

The Duke of Rothesay is Prince Charles, the heir to the British throne. In 1398, King Robert III of Scotland bestowed the title on his eldest son and it remains the premier Scottish title of the heir apparent. A royal charter was granted to the burgh of Rothesay in 1403; the charter was extended by James VI of Scotland (later James I of England) in 1584.

The arms of the Royal Burgh of Rothesay on a lamp-post

Left: Detail of an altar-tomb of a woman and child in St Mary's Chapel, Rothesay

Opposite: The Old Mansion House near Rothesay Castle, now used as offices by Bute Estates

17

A piece of sculpture from the doorway of St John's Church, now in the churchyard of the High Kirk, Rothesay

Left: Rothesay's golf course, on Canada Hill

library and museum in Rothesay are both worth a visit, and the key facility for visitors is, of course, the Tourist Information Centre.

Rothesay is busy in the summer season, sometimes positively teeming with tourists and yet a couple of miles outside the town there seems to be space to spare for everyone. Bute is a quiet and peaceful island, with much of interest for the antiquarian or naturalist. Many interesting and informative leaflets and guidebooks are available from the Tourist Information Centre in Rothesay or from Bute Museum.

There are plenty of opportunities for outdoor entertainment on Bute. Rothesay Golf Club has an eighteen-hole golf course and there are smaller courses at Port Bannatyne and Kingarth. There are pony-trekking centres, cycle-hiring companies, an excellent island bus service, regular coach tours from Rothesay and plenty of taxis for those visitors not content with exploring the island on foot.

North of Rothesay, near Port Bannatyne, is Kames Castle, a sixteenth-century tower house built on foundations as old as the fourteenth century. It housed the Bannatynes of Kames, chamberlains to the Stewart kings of Scotland when Bute was a royal demesne – part of the 'domain' of the Crown. The last of the line died in 1780. His nephew was the advocate who became Lord Kames in 1799, a founder member of the Bannatyne Club, which published an important series of books on Scottish history and literature.

Above and opposite: Ardencraig Gardens, above Craigmore Pier, Rothesay

The road system in the southern half of the island is complex, which only adds to the thrill of discovery and the joy of exploration. Basically a road runs round the coastline heading south out of Rothesay round Bogany Point, through Craigmore and Ardencraig to Ascog. Further on is Mount Stuart, home to the Marquess of Bute and now open to the public (enquire locally for opening hours). The Marquess of Bute was made the hereditary Keeper of Rothesay Castle in 1498. Today Historic Scotland, the government agency responsible for historic buildings, holds the keys to the castle but the Marquess still holds the honorary position of Keeper.

At the south-east corner of Bute is the wonderful Kilchattan Bay, with the remains of a medieval chapel and a safe sandy beach overlooked by the vitrified Iron Age hill-fort of Dunagoil. Just three miles to the east, in the Firth of Clyde, is the island of Great Cumbrae, with Little Cumbrae to its south.

Continuing round the coast, now heading north, the road runs up the west coast of Bute, with the little island of Inchmarnock coming into view. It is named after the same saint who is remembered in the industrial town of Kilmarnock, near Glasgow. St Marnoc is thought to have died in AD625. Inchmarnock lies about a mile (1.6km) offshore from St Ninian's Bay. During World War II (1939–45) the island was used for commando training,

THE CLYDE STEAMERS

Bute is an attractive little island, easily accessible from industrial Scotland, yet retaining many of the elements of Highland life, especially away from the tourist town of Rothesay.

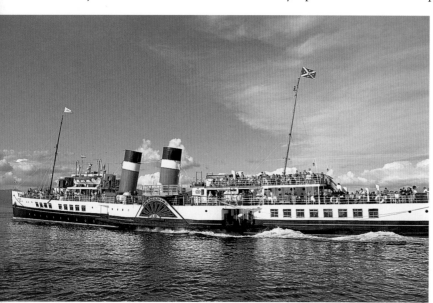

In the summer season, visitors can experience something of the excitement of past excursionists, as the last of the Clyde steamers, including the paddle-steamer Waverley, *ply for trade around the Clyde resorts and through the Kyles of Bute. With the Highland Line cutting through the middle of Bute, it is possible to experience both Highland and Lowland scenery in the space of a few miles.*

Opposite: Ascog Hall Fernery, restored to its late-Victorian splendour

but is now a peaceful spot again, with the largest herring gull colony in the Clyde. Archaeological finds from Inchmarnock show that warriors and priests have long shared this beautiful island – a rare Bronze Age crescentic jet necklace from Inchmarnock is on show in the Bute Museum in Rothesay.

St Ninian's chapel, on the island of Bute across from Inchmarnock, is likely to be one of the earliest Christian sites in Scotland. Ninian, who predated St Columba and is thought to have died in the first half of the sixth century, operated from his headquarters at Whithorn, in Wigtownshire. This corner of Bute is one of its most attractive and peaceful locations.

To the north of St Ninian's Bay is Ettrick Bay, from where a road crosses the island to Port Bannatyne and Rothesay. A minor road continues north from Ettrick Bay, hugging one of the arms of the Kyles of Bute and terminating at Kilmichael, with the remains of an early chapel, possibly destroyed by the Norsemen. Beyond Glecknabae, vehicle access is restricted to residents and farm traffic only.

The people of Bute are well accustomed to visitors and a friendly welcome is assured. The island is sheltered by neighbouring Arran and Kintyre from the worst of the weather, but good rain gear and adequate footwear are essential. The wind and rain can both be extremely penetrating, though in the tourist season bad weather does not generally last long – the gales blow it away in a day or two at most. In wet weather, there are castles, museums and great houses to visit, and the attractions of Rothesay to explore. Bute is a great place for walkers and cyclists, and is an excellent centre for an outdoor holiday. There are excellent local guidebooks for interested visitors, available from the Tourist Information Centre in Rothesay, and from other outlets.

The shoreline is always of interest, especially to children, and there are safe, sandy beaches. For less energetic visitors a car is a useful asset for exploring the island, but in this book we hope to encourage people to enjoy for themselves some of the fine walking possibilities of Bute, to see at first hand the archaeological and historical attractions in an interesting and scenically beautiful natural environment. Even in a small island there are scenic gems and surprises to be discovered, and while encouraging visitors to explore all the more accessible parts of the island, we leave open the possibilities for them to discover for themselves some of the nooks and crannies which Bute has to offer.

Looking south-east from Suidhe Chatain, the seat of St Catan, to the island of great Cumbrae and the mainland beyond

1 ROTHESAY – ISLAND CAPITAL

A FLUCTUATING POPULATION

A FLUCTUATING POPULATION

The following figures, taken from the 1991 Census, reveal the dominance of Rothesay on the island.

Rothesay	6,116
Port Bannatyne	682
Kilchattan Bay	153
Rural Bute	403
Total	7,354

The population figures shown below reflect variations in the island's economy over the last two centuries.

	Rothesay	Bute
1801	3,760	6,106
1851	7,104	9,386
1871	7,800	10,094
1891	9,108	11,753
1911	9,299	11,841
1931	9,347	12,126
1951	10,141	12,547
1971	6,456	8,141
1991	6,116	7,354

Pages 26–7: The view from near St Blane's chapel, Kingarth parish, looking across to Arran, with its Holy Isle visible on the horizon

ROTHESAY IS THE CAPITAL of Bute and the dominant factor in its economy. Of the total resident population of Bute, 6,116 out of 7,354 live in Rothesay (1991 Census). Other statistics gleaned from the 1991 Census show that 1 per cent of the population are Gaelic speakers, presumably from other parts of Scotland, 206 people were not born in the UK, and that 602 people were born in England. An analysis of the age profile of the population shows that 33 per cent are between age thirty-five and retirement age, 29 per cent are over retirement age, 20 per cent are between sixteen and thirty-four, and 18 per cent are under sixteen years of age.

Population figures for the burgh of Rothesay and the island of Bute over the years show the rise and fall of the island's fortunes.

From these numbers it will be evident that the older inhabitants of Bute must realise that the Bute of their childhood is gone for ever, and that the heyday of island tourism can never be regained. Bute must find the confidence to go into the next millennium as a smaller, yet equally vibrant, island community, with the collective knowledge and skills to make their smaller economy viable. After far too many years of depression and lack of confidence, at last it seems that today's islanders are beginning to find a way to stop the rot and regenerate their community.

The residents of Rothesay are proud to be able to say that they live in a Royal Burgh, granted by Robert III of Scotland at the royal castle of Rothesay on 12 January 1400. This protected the merchants of Rothesay by giving them a monopoly of all trade into and out of the town – 'strictly forbidding any extraneous merchant or such person whatsoever to buy or sell or use merchandise of any kind'. Subsequently, in 1584, James VI renewed the 1400 charter and granted Rothesay extensive maritime privileges over the waters of the Firth of Clyde and granted the Provost of Rothesay the title of 'Admiral of the Lower Reaches of the Clyde'.

The history of Rothesay, and indeed of the whole island of Bute, is linked very closely to Scotland's royal dynasty, the Stewarts. Their main fortress on Bute was the circular Rothesay Castle, the most important medieval building on the island and its main centre of power. The castle was originally built on a mound close to the sea, though with harbour and promenade improvements over the last two centuries it is now well inland and perhaps less impressive as a symbol of power and dominance over the local population.

The early history of Rothesay Castle is unclear, but it is quite probable that it was not, at the very beginning of its long history, a Scottish castle at all. In the early Middle Ages the Western Isles and parts of the furthest western coastal areas of the mainland of Scotland were conquered, occupied, settled and governed not by the kings of Scotland but by the kings of Norway.

Initial Viking raids in the Hebrides began around AD800 and Norway ruled the Western Isles by right until the Treaty of Perth in 1266 formally transferred sovereignty from Norway to Scotland. However, by the time of Somerled in the 1150s the island territories had effectively broken away from the rule of their Norse overlords, and his son Rognvald (Reginald) and grandson Domhnall (Donald) consolidated their position as the ruling dynasty of the semi-autonomous sea kingdom that became romantically known as the Lordship of the Isles.

For a hundred years before Somerled's successful rebellion in the 1150s, the Norsemen were aware of their deteriorating position in their western possessions and in the 1090s their king, Magnus Barefoot, led several expeditions to the Hebrides to reassert Norse control. These

Rothesay Castle and the County Buildings

Overleaf: Rothesay Castle, the island's royal power centre, surrounded by a moat

campaigns culminated in apparent success in 1098, when Norway and Scotland concluded a treaty allowing the Norse to retain unchallenged possession of all the islands off the west coast of Scotland which could be sailed around in a Norse longship, 'with the rudder set'. No doubt the Scottish king thought that the islands of Bute and Arran, protected from the west by the long peninsula of Kintyre, would be safe from these arrangements.

However, Magnus cunningly claimed Kintyre as one of his 'islands' by having a small galley dragged across the narrow isthmus at Tarbert, while seated at its stern and steering its rudder. He then circumnavigated Bute and Arran, and claimed both of them for Norway. It is thought that Rothesay Castle might have been established by Magnus at that time to enforce his claim.

Whoever was responsible for erecting the first fortress at Rothesay, it was not long before it became an important Scottish royal castle. It first came under Stewart control in 1164, when Somerled led his islesmen into a confrontation at Renfrew with the Scottish army. Somerled lost – either defeated in battle or killed by treachery, according to which chroniclers you read – and his armies retreated to their island homes. The Scottish king, Malcolm, gave Bute as a prize or reward to Walter Fitz Alan, the High Steward of Scotland, the head of the family which later became the royal Stewarts.

When the Norsemen attacked Rothesay in 1230, during an attempt to reassert their control over the islands which were still legally theirs, the action was so dramatic that it was preserved by one of the saga writers:

> And they sailed south round the Mull of Kintyre, and so in to Bute. The Scots sat there in the castle; and a certain steward was one of the Scots. They attacked the castle, but the Scots defended it, and they poured out boiling pitch. The Norwegians hewed the wall with axes, because it was soft. The torch-bearer who was called Skagi shot the steward to death. Many of the Norwegians fell, before they won the castle.

So the Norsemen prevailed in the end and captured Rothesay Castle from the Scots, killing its Steward in the process but losing many men themselves. After only a short occupation, the men of Norway withdrew to Kintyre, faced with a fleet of nearly 200 ships under Alan of Galloway.

In April 1398 King Robert III of Scotland conferred the hereditary title of Duke of Rothesay on his eldest son, David, in the royal castle in Rothesay. This honour continues to be held by the sovereign's eldest son and is currently held by Prince Charles. The 600th anniversary of this ceremony was celebrated in 1998, which was also the 500th anniversary of the creation of the honour of hereditary Captain and Keeper of Rothesay Castle, an honour still held by the Bute family. The post was created in 1498 when King James IV of Scotland appointed Ninian, the Sheriff of Bute and Arran, to this symbolically important position.

Rothesay Castle was occupied by Cromwellian forces during the civil wars of the 1650s; they are said to have demolished some of the defences

A gravestone in the churchyard of the High Kirk, Rothesay

when they departed in 1659. However, more serious damage was done in 1685, when Archibald, 9th Earl of Argyll, led a short-lived revolt, burning the castle and rendering it uninhabitable. It was at this time that the Keeper and his family moved from the now derelict castle to the Old Mansion House nearby on the High Street. The full history of Rothesay Castle, including an account of how it was restored by John Crichton Stuart, the 3rd Marquess of Bute, can be found in the Historic Scotland guidebook, available at the castle entrance. There is a small admission charge.

Rothesay Castle was placed in State care by the Marquess of Bute in 1961, and is now looked after by Historic Scotland on behalf of the Secretary of State for Scotland. Its complicated architecture, spiral stone staircases and dark dungeons can best be explored with the assistance of the excellent little guidebook sold on the premises. The central, circular courtyard, now grassed and empty but once teeming with the hustle and bustle of castle life, forms the core of the original stone castle, to which impressive towers and an even more impressive gateway were added over the centuries. The restored hall is used as an exhibition area where the history of the castle is explained. With its dark passages, battlements and stone-walled rooms, Rothesay Castle is a great place to explore on a rainy day, and a wonderful adventure for both children and adults. Its circular layout is unusual, but it is its sheer size and scale which is most impressive – truly a building of great prestige and power from which important agents of the Crown ruled their island estates.

The castellated frontage of the County Buildings and Prison near the castle, built in 1832

While our ancestors built the imposing County Buildings and Prison in 1832 on one side of the square surrounding Rothesay Castle and its moat, late twentieth-century architects have failed most notably on two other sides of the square. Beside the little gem of the Bute Museum is the abominable Moat Centre, a 1975 concrete pillbox containing a community centre and the public library. Inside, the library is pleasant, light and airy, with friendly, helpful staff, but the external appearance is depressing in the extreme. It looks across to the even more depressing telephone exchange and government buildings containing the tax office and job centre, all with architecture which could not be more ugly and unsuitable to complement the imposing castle walls.

Inside, both the library and museum are worth a visit. The library has an interesting local history collection, and a librarian with an encyclopaedic knowledge of the island. Some of the older books on the history of Bute are difficult to obtain elsewhere, and there is no better place to read up on the island than in this friendly library. There are also back files (with some gaps) of *The Buteman*, the island's newspaper founded in 1855, copies of the Censuses for the island parishes, 1841–81, old Parish Registers (for births, marriages and deaths before 1855) and the Mormon IGI (International Genealogical Index) to help historical and family history researchers.

The Bute Museum, unusual in being purpose built in 1927 by its patron, the 4th Marquess of Bute for the Buteshire Natural History Society,

Bute Museum, built in 1927 to display the collections of the Buteshire National History Society

is another ideal destination for a rainy day, but is such an important repository of the island's history that it should be visited even on the sunniest of days, rather than not at all! The industrial history of Bute is well represented, from traditional farming and fishing to cotton mills, tileworks, brickworks and of course the Rothesay Tramways Company which ran to Port Bannatyne and Ettrick Bay from 1902 until superseded by motor buses in 1935. Bute was greatly affected by World War II and the Museum reflects its military occupation by naval forces from many countries. Most importantly, HMS *Cyclops*, the depot ship for the 7th Submarine Flotilla, was based in Rothesay Bay, while from 1942 the Kyles of Bute Hydro was the headquarters of the 12th Submarine Flotilla, HMS *Varbel*, specialising in midget submarines and human torpedoes. The name was derived from combining elements of the names of Commander C. Varley, DSO, RN, who evolved the midget sub and Commander T. Bell, DSC, RN, who was in charge of training operations in Loch Striven. Apart from operations against the battleship *Tirpitz* in 1942 and 1943, men of this unusual unit sunk the Italian cruiser *Ulpio Traiano* in Palermo harbour and the 10,000 ton cruiser *Bolzano* at La Spetzia. Three VCs were awarded. Thirty-nine officers and men were killed during wartime operations.

The putting green at the Winter Garden

Of great interest are the photographic collections in the Bute Museum, which will bring back many memories of the past for both islanders and visitors alike. These cover more recent events too, like the serious floods in Rothesay in 1991 and the demolition of the Bute Arms Hotel, the first temptation for generations of visitors arriving by steamer. Built on reclaimed land facing the harbour, its foundations were insecure and a large empty square now welcomes today's visitors.

The archaeological and prehistoric collections in the Bute Museum are of national importance and include an excellent example of a crescent-shaped necklace of jet-black beads found in a Bronze Age cist (burial chamber) on the island of Inchmarnock in 1961, alongside the skeleton of a woman, and her equally prized flint knife blade. The necklace is made of 135 beads of jet, a material related to lignite and most probably obtained, through trade, from a source at Whitby in Yorkshire. A similar necklace from a cist at Mount Stuart excavated in 1887 is in the National Museum of Scotland in Edinburgh. Jet necklaces are characteristic of female Bronze Age burials, presumably of aristocratic women, and are likely to be at least 3,500 years old. Other display cases in the Bute Museum contain prehistoric pottery and artefacts from sites throughout the island. There is a small admission charge. The Museum is staffed by volunteers from the Buteshire Natural History Society, who operate a small shop selling island souvenirs and produce a useful range of publications, including six leaflets guiding visitors around Rothesay and different parts of the island of Bute. They deserve to be supported.

The Inchmarnock jet necklace, displayed in Bute Museum

Adjacent to the pier is the Winter Garden of 1924, also recently restored to its original splendour after a period of decay. It houses a cinema and an excellent restaurant and is well used for public meetings and functions. The iron and glass building is decorated in the Art Nouveau style. In its heyday it was the venue for all the famous Music Hall entertainers of the day. By contrast, the Rothesay Pavilion, further along the esplanade, reflects the 1930s taste for abstract design. It was built as a dance hall, concert hall and restaurant, and is still very much in use. The new pier buildings were opened in 1968 by the Queen Mother – the old pier building, with its landmark clock tower, burned down in 1962. Photographs of this sad event can be seen in the Bute Museum, but the new building does manage to capture the spirit of the old central clock tower in its modern functional design. The ferry company, Caledonian MacBrayne, has its offices in the new pier buildings (tel: 01700 502707).

The Old Mansion House, once the town house of the Stewarts of Bute, now estate offices for Bute Estates

There are many other interesting and attractive buildings in Rothesay, ranging from the Old Mansion House near the castle, once the town residence of the Marquesses of Bute and now the office for Bute Estates, to the tenements of the town centre and the sometimes rather grand mansions and villas which were the holiday houses for wealthy Glasgow businessmen. Unfortunately, many of the buildings in Rothesay are rather run down and in need of repair and restoration, having been sadly neglected as the island's

TEMPLE OF CONVENIENCE

After this whirlwind tour of the literary, historical and cultural treasures of Bute, it may seem a little unusual to direct visitors to a Gents' Toilet, but no visit to Rothesay is complete without a visit to the Victorian Toilets on Rothesay Pier. Restored to full working splendour by the Strathclyde Building Preservation Trust at a cost of almost £300,000, these 'jewels in the sanatarian's crown' were officially re-opened in 1994 when a section was added for ladies – the needs of Victorian ladies were not recognised so publicly. However, the curiosity of modern ladies is catered for, according to a sign at the entrance: 'Visitors, especially female visitors, are offered the opportunity to view the Gents at the following times: 10am, 1pm, 4pm'. Male visitors can of course gain access at any time during opening hours (Easter to October 8am–9pm; November to March, 9am–5pm).

The interior décor of this Victorian gem is nothing short of splendiferous. Green marble splendour, decorative white ceramic tiles, a floor of ceramic mosaic, glass-sided cisterns and gleaming copper plumbing make it clear that the first impression the Royal Burgh of Rothesay wished to convey to its male visitors was the best that Twyford's Ltd could supply – at a cost in 1899 of £530. The trade name for these top-of-the-range public urinals is imprinted in the white fireclay of every stall – the 'Adamant'. Definitely not to be missed.

economy suffered. The decline of mass tourism in Bute, with the Glaswegian hordes opting for the delights of Majorca and Corfu, has meant a reassessment of island life. The Bute Housing Association is involved in the renovation and refurbishment of old properties, but though it has achieved much, much remains to be done. It is sad to see so many empty and derelict commercial properties in the town; it is to be hoped that the efforts to develop and enhance the island's major industry – tourism – will result in the regeneration of Rothesay as traders realise that the island's main hope is to attract more discriminating tourists to the town, and to provide them with the goods and services they have come to expect.

There is also a great need to extend the tourist season by marketing the natural attractions of the landscape and natural environment of Bute, which can be enjoyed at any time of the year. Perhaps there is less need for the more than twenty cafés which provide a welcome cup of tea at peak times during the height of summer, and more need for more 'quality' establishments which today's more pampered visitors have come to expect, and which off-season visitors would appreciate.

One establishment which is justly famous for its culinary delights is the West End Café, which has won awards for being the best fish and chip shop in Scotland. Rothesay café society is dominated by the Zavaroni clan, part of that sub-culture of Italian cafés which was such a feature of west of Scotland life even before World War I, and which survived some regrettable and unjustified attacks by local zealots at the beginning of World War II. The most famous member of the Rothesay Zavaroni family is Lena, who belted out hit singles at a tender age in the 1960s and became a household name.

There are one or two manifestations of local government zeal which deserve mention. Beside the Winter Garden is an attractive wrought iron arch, surmounted by an attractive view of a Highland scene, complete with deer, heather, lochs and mountains, and the legend: 'Welcome to the Highlands. You are standing on the Highland Boundary Fault'. Go through the arch and look back and the scene is now somewhere in the Lowlands, with rolling hills, fields and a grazing milk cow: 'Welcome to the Lowlands. You are standing on the Highland Boundary Fault'. Simple, attractive, clever and informative. Further information on the geology of Bute can be found in the Bute Museum.

By contrast, at the back of the new square facing the harbour, where once the Bute Arms Hotel stood, is a gap site in a row of nineteenth-century buildings, now occupied by a black metal contraption on which banners are hung during the summer months, in front of which is a row of rather sad-looking conifers in large pots. It appears that the local Bute Partnership paid rather a large amount of money for this example of civic art, but perhaps its continued presence is sufficient embarrassment without revealing further details here. At least the attempt to fill the derelict space was commendable, though the end result is not to everybody's taste.

Continuing out of the High Street past the castle and the police station is the route leading along the line of Loch Fad, along the Highland Boundary Fault, to the west side of Bute. On the outskirts of the town are the Creamery (a cheese-making establishment offering visitor tours, with a factory shop selling island cheese), the hospital, leisure complex with swimming pool, and St Mary's church and graveyard, the site of Rothesay's medieval parish church. In the chapel building, restored by Historic Scotland, are medieval tombs and grave slabs.

For visitors, undoubtedly the most important building in Rothesay is the Tourist Information Centre, facing the harbour (tel: 01700 502151). Here can be found a comprehensive collection of books, leaflets, brochures and maps relating to Bute, with helpful and informed staff prepared to help with accommodation and other arrangements.

The tomb of a medieval knight in St Mary's Chapel

Cheese-making at Rothesay Creamery

37

2 THE NORTH END

ALTHOUGH THE QUICKEST AND easiest way to get to Bute is by the fast, efficient and frequent car ferries from Wemyss Bay to Rothesay, visitors bringing their own cars to the island may wish to approach by the alternative ferry route, across the Kyles of Bute from Colintraive to Rhubodach (pronounced with the accent on the middle syllable: 'roo-BO-dach'). The journey from Glasgow to Colintraive is eighty miles in length, requiring the best part of two hours, but it is through some of the most glorious scenery in Scotland. The route from Glasgow leads through Dumbarton, up the west shore of Loch Lomond, through the village of Arrochar at the head of Loch Long, and into Argyll under the watchful eye of The Cobbler. Then, over the Rest and Be Thankful Pass to the Dunoon road end, just before the village of Cairndow, and down through Strachur and the middle of the district of Cowal, through Glendaruel to the Kyles of Bute and the ferry slip at Colintraive. The ferry operates continuously throughout the day; the journey is quick (5 minutes) and cheap. Visitors not used to this route should watch the road signs carefully, or they are likely to end up either in Dunoon or Tighnabruaich.

Apart from economic considerations, one reason for this approach to Bute is that it gives travellers time to leave their urban environment behind and to adjust to a different way of life. In many ways Rothesay is no more 'typical' of Bute than Torremolinos is of southern Spain; indeed, in Victorian guidebooks, Rothesay was described as 'the Madeira of Scotland' and as the era of the Mediterranean packaged holiday got under way, as 'the Costa Clyde'. Writing in the *New Statistical Account*, in 1840, the Reverend Robert Craig, minister of the parish, described Rothesay as 'the Montpellier of Scotland', where 'the winter snows are hardly ever known to lie above a day or two unmelted; and ever-green plants, which thrive admirably here, are seldom or ever injured by the frosts.' Reverend Craig goes on to sing the praises of the island's climate: 'such is the mildness and salubrity of the climate, that many persons affected with consumption, asthma, and rheumatism derive the greatest benefit from a winter residence in the island'.

Left: The journey from Glasgow to Bute follows the west shore of Loch Lomond. Here, the pier at Luss, on Loch Lomond, is overlooked by Ben Lomond

Overleaf: Balnakailly Bay at the north end of Bute, looking across the Kyles of Bute to the Cowal hills

VIGBIOD AND VESTMAR

In the 870s, two Vikings named Vigbiod and Vestmar, described in Grettis Saga as natives of the Hebrides, got a bit of a reputation for unnecessary and excessive plundering in Ireland, in the Hebrides, and 'in Scotland's firths'. Two well-behaved Vikings called Thrond and Onund were sent to rein them in. Onund was famous for his wooden leg. The saga describes how Vigbiod and Vestmar were cornered off 'the island which is called Bute' and says that 'there was a great channel there and deep, and ships could sail one way only, and not more than five at a time'. A battle ensued, Onund pretended to be trapped in the narrows, and lured his enemies' boats under a cliff, from where his followers hurled stones at them. Finding themselves trapped by the narrowness of the Kyles, and unable to retreat against the current, Vigbiod and Vestmar were defeated. Onund himself was in a sword-fight with Vigbiod.

> *Then his sword struck into the log that Onund had under his knee, and the sword stuck fast. Vigbiod stooped as he pulled his sword to him; upon this, Onund struck him on the shoulder and took off his arm. Then the viking was out of the battle. When Vestmar knew that his companion had fallen, he leapt into the ship that lay farthest out, and fled; so did all they that could.*

(continued opposite)

Despite its long and proud history, Rothesay as it appears today is a holiday town, its holiday villas, tenements and cafés more reminiscent of an amalgamation of Glasgow societies. By arriving at Rhubodach the visitor is immediately introduced to traditional Bute, with the road to Rothesay running along the shores of the Kyles of Bute on a raised beach, past a scatter of farms. No cars are allowed north of Rhubodach (Gaelic: *Rudha-Mhodach*, Bute point), though a track leads to Balnakailly Bay (Gaelic: *Baile-na-choille*, the township of the wood), which is a good place to observe wildlife on and around the little islands in the Kyles of Bute, the Burnt Islands – Eilean Fraoich, Eilean Mor and Eilean Buidhe (in Gaelic, the heather island, the big island and the yellow island). It is possible to walk round the inelegantly named Buttock Point, the most northerly point of Bute, to admire the Maids of Bute, two painted rocks perhaps best observed from the sea, or from the Tighnabruaich shore in Cowal. According to Neil Munro the first person to paint these stones was Peter Macfarlane, 'Para Handy':

> . . . I never had no education at drawin', and it's wonderful how fine I pented them. When you got close to them they were no more like rale maids than I am; . . . but before I wass done with them, ye would ask them up to dance . . . The North end o' Bute iss a bleak, wild, lonely place, but when I wass done pentin' the Maids it looked like a large population . . . Och! but it wass chust imachination; when we pass the Maids o' Bute now, I know they're only stones, with rud and white paint on them. They're good enough for towerists!

They are still there, and still good enough for today's 'towerists' (tourists). Neil Munro's *Para Handy Tales*, first published in 1955 and widely available in reprinted paperback format, is an excellent introduction to a way of life which once prevailed in all the nooks and crannies of the Firth of Clyde frequented by the *Vital Spark* in its literary voyages.

Just over four miles south of Rhubodach the road leaves the shore, cutting across the wide and flat expanse of Ardmaleish Point. It rejoins the coast at Kames Bay (Gaelic: *camas*, bay), passes the turnings to Kames Castle and to Ettrick Bay, and arrives at the village of Port Bannatyne. Taking its name from the landed gentry of Kames Castle, Port Bannatyne was known throughout the Clyde and far beyond for McIntyre's boatbuilding yard, famous equally for its Loch Fyne skiffs (small fishing boats) and racing yachts. There was another boatyard at Ardmeleish. Servicing and repair of yachts and small boats is still an important local industry. A few shops, tea-rooms and pubs along the sea-front at Port Bannatyne are but a hint of how busy this place was in its heyday.

The waters around Bute are particularly enjoyable for the yachting fraternity. Sailing in the sheltered waters of the Kyles, or anchoring in some of the bays, or watching the seals on the offshore islands between Colintraive and Rhubodach – these are memorable experiences.

Kames Castle, a fourteenth-century tower house surrounded by later farm buildings

Port Bannatyne merges into Ardbeg and within a further two miles the shore road arrives in the centre of Rothesay itself, just over 8 miles (13km) from the ferry at Rhubodach. Ardbeg is almost entirely residential, with just a couple of local shops. The houses, cottages and villas on the sea-front here are much sought after, many offering bed-and-breakfast accommodation in the summer season.

Returning to Kames Bay, a good road leads across the narrow waist of Bute to Ettrick Bay, a distance of just over two miles. Just after leaving the junction at Kames Bay, Kames Castle comes into view on the north side of the road. This castle is in private grounds and is *not* open to the public, but because it has played such an important part in the history of Bute it is worth describing it briefly. Kames Castle is a massive fourteenth-century keep, four storeys high, with a crenellated parapet. It was originally surrounded by a moat, of which only traces remain. Later farm and estate buildings now surround the stone keep. The walls were 6ft (2m) thick, with the building itself measuring 36 x 26ft (11 x 8m). Much of the original structure remains, though there has been some restoration.

(continued)
In the aftermath of this skirmish, Osmund found Vigbiod bleeding to death and could not resist gloating: 'The one-legged warrior got from thee no scratch. To many a fighter is more boastfulness given than wisdom: the warrior is without strength in danger.

More important than the architecture of their typical fourteenth-century fortified house, was the family which occupied it, the ancient family of Bannatyne, originally from Ayrshire. Gilbert, and his son John, were granted charters to Kames from Walter the High Steward of Scotland, the son-in-law of Robert the Bruce. The family sent four sons to the disastrous battle of Flodden in 1513, at which King James IV and much of the Scottish nobility were killed. In 1594 Kames is mentioned by Dean Munro as one of the two castles on Bute – the other one being at Rothesay, or 'Rosay'. Hector

Bronze Age stones near St Colmac, the remains of a stone circle

Bannatyne of Kames was a member of the Scottish Parliament from 1617 to 1639, and in 1704 another Hector was Commissioner of Supply for Buteshire, an important local government post. At one time the family had eleven estates throughout Scotland, though Kames was always the main one. The last of the direct line of Bannatynes was James, who died unmarried in 1786, at the age of eighty-nine. He was succeeded by his nephew William Macleod, who took the name of Bannatyne. He was an important Scottish advocate (lawyer), made a judge in 1799 with the title Lord Kames, and knighted. Lord Kames was one of the leading members of the Bannatyne Club, a group of antiquarians who published important Scottish historical material. He died in 1833, aged ninety-one, but unfortunately lost his fortune and had to sell Kames in 1812. Since then it has been in a succession of private ownerships.

Within the estate of Kames is a smaller fortified house of the sixteenth century, once completely ruinous but now restored and modernised. This tiny castle measures only 25 x 21ft (7.5 x 6.5m). In the fourteenth century, in the time of Robert the Bruce, the lands of Wester Kames belonged to a MacKinlay family, whose three sons were expert archers. In an archery contest at Rothesay Castle they had the misfortune to defeat the king's archers, who subsequently sought to raid the house of their conquerors. Unfortunately the MacKinlay sons killed seventeen of them, which irritated the king so much that he ordered the family out, and gave the property to his butler, or dispenser (ie, Spenser), a MacDonald. His descendants took the name Spens, and called their lairdship the House of Spens. In 1670 their little castle passed by marriage to the Grahams, and eventually, like most of the island, to the Stuarts of Bute. The Spens family were thus important in Bute for 350 years and appear frequently in the historical record.

Half-way to Ettrick Bay, the roofless church of St Colmac and its graveyard are worth a visit. Across the road, in a field, the remains of a Bronze Age stone circle, dating from before 1500BC, lie in a small circular plantation of trees.

Ettrick Bay is a much more 'Hebridean' beach than the gravelly Kames Bay or the reddish Old Red Sandstone sand of Kilchattan Bay in the south

of the island. The sands of Ettrick Bay are white and fine, and it's a wonderful place for a picnic or a long walk on the beach. The meaning of this place-name is debated among experts, but a likely possibility is that it is a Gaelic–Norse hybrid, from Gaelic: *eathar*, a small boat, and Norse: *vik*, a bay. The beach itself is almost exactly one mile long, and eminently suitable for beaching small boats. There is a telephone kiosk and a seasonal tea-room at the north end of Ettrick Bay, and a large car park to accommodate summer day trippers. This is also the best place to park for walkers interested in ascending Windy Hill, 912ft (278m).

Just before Ettrick Bay a road turns off to the north, up Glen More, but it is not suitable or appropriate for visitors to take vehicles up this road and it is best to park at Ettrick Bay. The track giving access to the hills and moors leads north from the farm of Upper Ettrick. Although Scottish hill-walkers determinedly defend their 'right to roam', Bute is an intensively farmed island and it is only courteous to enquire at local farms if there is any reason not to traverse the lower fields which give access to the hills.

Leaving the car park at Ettrick Bay, it is possible to drive for a further two miles, round Kildavanan Point, up the west coast of Bute to the farm of Glecknabae (Gaelic: *Gleuc-na-Beithe*, the glen or hollow of the birches). Kildavanan is Gaelic: *Cill-da-Mhanan*, the 'cell' or church of Adamnan, who was the abbot of Iona one hundred years after the death of St Columba and who was the author of that saint's biography. *Kil-* names are always an indication of an early Christian presence, and this example at Kildavanan is no exception. Christianity first came to this part of Scotland in the sixth century, in the time of Ninian, Columba, Ciaran, and numerous other saints, most of whom came over from Ireland as part of a settlement of Gaelic-speaking peoples into Argyll and adjacent islands. This 'Celtic' Christianity operated on the fringes of Christendom, largely independent of Rome, though after the Synod of Whitby (AD664) it followed the same practices (as, for example, when calculating the date of Easter) as the rest of the church.

Soon after AD800 Viking raiders began looting and ravaging early Christian monasteries throughout the Western Isles and it must be presumed that Bute was not immune from their attentions. In some places Christianity was almost obliterated, but there is plenty of evidence, especially after the conversion of Norway to Christianity in AD1000, that Odin and the Christian God co-existed satisfactorily, if not always happily. However, until the Treaty of Perth (1266) Bute, like all the Norse territories, was technically administered in the ecclesiastical realm by the Bishop of Trondheim, in Norway.

A broken cross-head from Inchmarnock, now in Edinburgh in the National Museum of Scotland, is a tangible example of a Christian cross from the time of the Norse occupation of Bute, for it has on it an inscrip-

Riders on the sands at Ettrick Bay

VIKING RAIDS

*Vikings first started raiding the
Western Isles and coasts of Scotland
around AD800. At first they went
for the easy pickings of Hebridean
monasteries, slaughtering monks
and stealing their precious religious
objects.*

*From Iona to Ireland, from
Caithness and Wester Ross to the
Kyles of Bute, they systematically
almost eradicated Christianity in
the parts of Scotland exposed to
their attacks. Later, they brought
their wives and children, settling in
lands less densely populated than
the pockets of fertile land around
their home fjords. For 350 years, the
Norse ruled the Hebrides, Orkney,
Shetland, Caithness and
Sutherland, as well as most of the
western coastal fringe of Scotland
from Wester Ross to the Mull of
Kintyre, and the Clyde islands of
Bute, Arran and Cumbrae.*

*Norse direct control ended with
Somerled's revolt in the 1150s, but
legal sovereignty of the Western
Isles, including Bute, lasted until
the Treaty of Perth in 1266.*

tion in runes, the distinctive, spidery alphabet which the Viking raiders, and the later Norse settlers, brought with them from Norway, just as the Gaels in the sixth century had brought their unique ogham script. The runic inscription of the Inchmarnock cross is fragmentary, but enough remains to be deciphered as, 'this cross [is erected] to Guthleif' [or Guthleik]: . . . KRUS.THINE.TIL GUTHLE . . .'

There are several Norse place-names on Bute, and we know the name of at least one other Norseman, for 'Rothesay' was originally not the name of the town but was the Norse name for the island itself – *Rothirs-ay*, Rothir's island. It is possible that this is a version of the man named Rudri or Ruadri or *Ruthri* who is mentioned in *Haakon's Saga* in connection with the invasion by Uspak, King of Man and the Isles, on behalf of Haakon IV of Norway in 1230. The language of the saga is dramatic, if not always easy to understand – even in translation:

King Haakon sent a light ship south to Bute in advance, to those whom the king had sent there, because he was long in getting a fair wind. The news there was that they had gained the castle; in this way, that those that were stationed in it had yielded it up, and had taken truce from the Norwegians.

There was a certain ship's commander whose name was Ruadri. He thought that he had an hereditary right to Bute. And because he had not got the island from the Scots, he had made great dispeace there, and had slain many men; and for this he was outlawed by the Scottish king. He came to king Haakon, and swore him oaths, and became his man; and his two brothers with him. And as soon as those that had given up the castle were away from the Norwegians, Ruadri slew nine of them, because he thought that no truce had been promised them. After this, the island of Bute was laid under king Haakon, as is here said:

'the renowned and unsparing company of the peace-breaker won
broad Bute from the god-hated ring users [ie, 'unlucky princes'];
the raven moved his wing's cloven sword over the vulture's feast,
in the Hebrides; the rulers' enemies fell.'

The Norwegians who were in Bute went ashore in Scotland, and burned a certain village, and many towns. Ruadri went far and wide, and did all the evil that he could.

This is the rascal after whom Rothesay is perhaps named! Some scholars point to his claim to Bute and speculate that he may even have been the grandson of the mighty Somerled himself.

In records of 1321 the spelling 'Rothersay' was used, though by 1400 it was 'Rosay', which is very close to the common local pronunciation today. In Gaelic, Rothesay was always *Baile Bhoid*, the town of Bute. The name of Bute itself is not easily deciphered. In a Norse saga of 1093 the island is called Bot, and it may have a connection with the trading booths or huts which probably grew up as soon as the Norse arrived in Rothesay Bay. Other authorities point out the Old Irish word *bot*, meaning a beacon fire and derive the name of the island from this meaning. Still others wonder if there may not be a survival of the name of the island in the Dark Ages, when its native Pictish inhabitants had as yet no contact with either Gaelic or Norse speakers.

North of Glecknabae is excellent for walking or cycling, but visitors should not attempt to take their cars further – a car park is provided and signs erected which make this clear. The track continues for a further two miles, past Kilmichael, another early Christian site with a chapel well worth a visit. Above Kilmichael farm is the important chambered cairn of Glenvoidean, excavated by Dorothy N. Marshall and other members of the Buteshire Natural History Museum. It was built, as a community burial place, at least 4,500 years ago; the finds from the excavations are in the Bute Museum. Three chambers, the forecourt and side walling of the cairn are all clearly visible.

This corner of Bute was important to Bute's first farmers – the Neolithic folk who brought agriculture, pottery and polished stone axes to the island. There are four large chambered cairns within two miles of each other, between Glecknabae and Kilmichael, so a visit to these sites would make an interesting half-day excursion for anybody with an interest in pre-history and archaeology. Of course, there is plenty of evidence of Neolithic activity in other parts of Bute and it may be that these great communal tombs have survived best in the north-west corner of Bute simply because it is less cultivated and so less damaged archaeologically than some of the more intensively cultivated and more fertile parts of the island, which must surely have been attractive to the early farmers.

The excavator at Glenvoidean chambered cairn, Dorothy Marshall, was for many years the mainstay of the Buteshire Natural History Society. She learned her archaeological trade digging at Jericho with Kathleen Kenyon, and at the Institute of Archaeology in London, but returned to Bute and throughout her long life carried out extensive surveys of both the archaeology and natural history of the island. Born in January 1900, she died in 1992, in her ninety-third year. Throughout the rather cosy world of Scottish archaeology, Dorothy Marshall was synonymous with Bute. It was a tribute both to her and to the wonderful archaeology of the island that so many professional archaeologists from Scotland's universities and museums found their way to Bute and offered their professional services to the local society. She was often to be seen at archaeological conferences and contributed articles on her work in Bute to the *Proceedings of the Society of Antiquaries of Scotland*, of which she was, of course, a Fellow. Dorothy Marshall's *History of Bute*, first published in 1950 and most recently revised in 1992, is an excellent introduction to the island and can be purchased in Bute Museum, and at other outlets. It is particularly useful for giving National Grid References for archaeological sites, and advice on access to sites.

NEOLITHIC CAIRNS

The chambered cairns of Bute and the rest of Scotland were built by the first farmers to settle in the landscape after the end of the Ice Age. From before 3500BC, and for almost 2,000 years thereafter, they cut down forests with their stone axes, lived in circular huts, grew cereal crops and raised sheep, cattle, pigs and goats. In upland Britain they buried their dead – or at least their ruling aristocracy – in stone chambers which they then covered with heaps of stones. These communal burial cairns were used again and again through the centuries. In lowland Britain, long barrows of earth and turf are the equivalent of the stone burial cairns found throughout Scotland.

In the second millennium BC they were succeeded by the first Celts, who were more warlike and had a knowledge of metal-working. In the Bronze Age the folk made tools of copper and bronze, built standing stones and stone circles, and buried their dead, often cremated, in small, circular stone cairns.

In the Iron Age, soon after 1000BC, a new culture emerged, with a knowledge of iron-working for swords and ploughshares, and the construction of hill-forts for defence.

There is much overlapping of these cultures, in both time and space, and it is by no means clear that whole populations were expelled and replaced by succeeding cultures. In many ways, the way of life in Bute in the eighteenth century was unchanged for perhaps 3,000 years.

3 THE EAST COAST

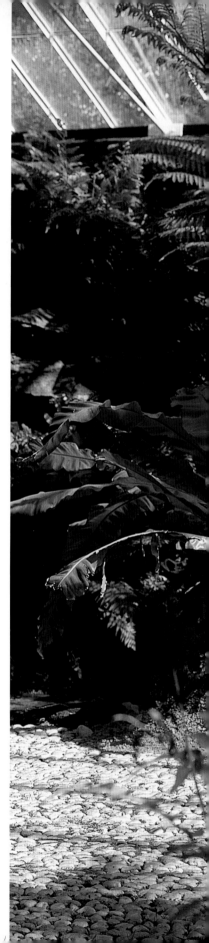

L EAVING ROTHESAY ALONG THE coast road to Kingarth and Kilchattan Bay, the route passes many attractive houses and hotels facing the sea, with further residences perched higher up. Some are splendid examples of Victorian architecture, notably the wedding cake tower of the Glendale Hotel and the cast-iron framework of an apartment building further along the esplanade. In Battery Place, the building with a classical frontage was built as an aquarium, later used as a swimming pool, and now awaits some appropriate use. High above the coastal strip is the massive Glenburn Hotel, built as a luxury hotel but now run mainly for the benefit of coach parties.

Rounding Barony Point, note the former Craigmore Pier building, now a restaurant. One of the roads leading up from the shore is signposted for Ardencraig Gardens, run by the local council and renowned, in the summer months, for its floral displays. From here there are various possibilities for walks: back into Rothesay through Skipper Wood, or up to Canada Hill, with spectacular views of the Firth of Clyde, supposedly taking its name from where families could catch a last glimpse of emigrant ships carrying relatives across to North America.

Nearly three miles out of Rothesay is Ascog Point (Norse: *askr-vik*, small-boat bay). The name is the same as at Port Askaig in Islay, in another island settled by the Norsemen. The *-aig* ending in place-names is usually taken as a Gaelic version of the Norse *vik*, a bay. An older Norse word, *ask-r*, means an ash tree, so an alternative is 'ash-tree bay'. At Ascog, an imposing white entrance arch announces 'The Railway Convalescent Home' (closed in 1997) and next door is the Ascog Hall Fernery and Gardens. This is a Victorian sunken fern house, built around 1870 with a glazed iron roof. It has no heating, but relies on Bute's mild climate and the fact that it is largely underground to protect its contents from occasional frosts. After a long period of neglect it was rescued in 1986, restored to its former glory, and opened to the public. It houses well over one hundred sub-tropical ferns from Australia, New Zealand, Fiji, Mauritius and Mexico – some of them very rare and unusual for this country.

During the research for the restoration, an inventory of the species originally installed in the fernery in the 1870s was found, and from this list

Ascog Hall Fernery, built by Alexander Bannatyne Stewart in the 1870s

50

plants were obtained from the Royal Botanic Gardens in Edinburgh, and the fernery exhibits reconstructed. One of the exhibits, a *Todea barbara*, is reputed to be 1,000 years old. Originally from Australia or New Zealand, this is one of the original plants collected for his summer house by A. B. Stewart, an important Glasgow businessman who was Convener of the County of Bute and maintained his Bute connections. Observant visitors will already have met this gentleman in the middle of Rothesay, beside the Winter Garden, where his statue was erected on his death in 1880, with the following inscription:

> Alexander Bannatyne Stewart
> Convener of the County of Bute
> b. 30th October 1836
> d. 27th May 1880
> Erected in affectionate remembrance
> of his public services and benefactions
> to the County of Bute
> and Royal Burgh of Rothesay

The fernery is situated in attractive gardens and is an unusual and delightful place to visit. There is a small admission charge.

A mile further on, continuing along the raised beach, the road reaches Kerrycroy, an estate village designed to make the English wife of the 2nd Marquess of Bute feel less homesick. Kerrycroy is one of several places in Bute with the *kerry-* element in their names. It is the Gaelic *ceathramh*, a quarter (of the pennyland division of land), pronounced 'ker-ruv'. Kerrycroy is 'the hard quarter' (Gaelic: *cruaidh*, hard). On the shore just to the north of the village are a couple of glacial erratics nestling on top of the local Old Red Sandstone bedrock.

The road to Rothesay – and Rothesay! – from Kilchattan Bay

Here the main road turns inland, to bypass the Mount Stuart estate, to which we shall return. The road passes through fertile Lowland scenery, for here we are on the southern side of the Highland Boundary Fault. The landscape is similar to that of the south end of Arran, or the southern tip of the Kintyre peninsula, or the coasts of Renfrewshire and Ayrshire across the Firth of Clyde – all with similar geology. Just over three miles from Kerrycroy we reach Kingarth and Kilchattan Bay. Kingarth (Gaelic: *ceann garadh*, head of the enclosure or yard) is one of the oldest documented place-names on Bute. It appears as Cindgaradh in one of the early Irish annals in AD737.

There is an old inn at the main road junction in Kingarth, at which one of the three signs on the signpost points to Kilchattan Bay, and the other two, pointing in opposite directions, to Rothesay! This is of course accurate, if not entirely helpful. Kilchattan Bay itself has pink sands, a row of houses and a hotel. It is a delightful place to potter about in for a day, exploring the beach, or as the beginning point of a walk round the south-

ern headlands of Bute. It takes its name from yet another early Christian saint, Catan, reputedly the uncle of St Blane.

In the 1840s, Kilchattan Bay was a quiet fishing village of about fifty small cottages – a remote, picturesque backwater. A fifteenth-century meal mill there was in use until the 1880s. There were three schools in the parish, six ale-houses, and a population of about 800. In 1849 a tileworks was built, which provided employment for twenty men and lasted until 1915. But, in the last quarter of the nineteenth century, Kilchattan Bay became a tourist resort, with its own pier and hotel and steamer services connecting it to Wemyss Bay, Fairlie and Millport. Villas and tenements were built and an anchorage provided for small boats. Tourism and agriculture are now the only occupations.

In early times this was one of the most populous areas of Bute. A charter of 1506 from James IV gave tenants rights and protections; most of the farm names mentioned in this document persist to the present day. One of the oldest surviving families in this part of Bute were the McCaws of Garrochty, who maintained their independence of the Stewarts of Bute until 1845, while most of their neighbours were taken over by the Bute Estate. At the south end of the village is Hawk's Neb Point, where 200-million-year-old fossil fishes have been found.

4 THE SOUTH END

A LITTLE TO THE WEST of the Kingarth crossroads, a minor road leads off to the south, signposted for St Blane's church and monastery. Beside this road, on the edge of a forestry plantation are three weathered standing stones, part of what was once a stone circle, dating from the Bronze Age (before 1500BC). In its Bronze Age archaeology Bute seems to have more in common with the neighbouring island of Arran, with its concentration of standing stones and stone circles at Machrie Moor, than with the mainland Argyll districts of Cowal and Kintyre, where standing stones are common but stone circles rare.

Between the Kingarth stone circle and the sea you may see a windsock fluttering in the breeze, marking an airstrip. South from the farms of Largizean (Gaelic: *Largihean*, the daisy field) and Lubas (Gaelic: *Lub-eas*, the bend of a waterfall), the Plan road heads for the hill named Suidhe Bhlain – St Blane's seat. This hill overlooks the early Christian monastery and chapel, and medieval chapel, which bear the name of St Blane, another early Christian saint. Car parking is provided at the end of the Plan road – vehicles should not proceed through the farm gates leading to

Standing stones in a clearing in the Black Park plantation, Kingarth, the remnants of a Bronze Age stone circle

Opposite: St Blane's chapel, Kingarth parish, the site of an early Christian monastery founded in the sixth century

Plan Farm and Garrochty Farm (Gaelic: *Garbh thidh*, the rough or rocky end; or perhaps *Garbh ach tigh*, house of the rough field). In the 1506 charter it was 'Garachach'. Plan Farm may be the only place-name on Bute with a Latin derivation, from *planum*, a plain.

A visit to St Blane's chapel is undoubtedly one of the highlights of a visit to Bute. From the road end it is an easy walk of no more than ten minutes and well worth the minimal effort involved. The site is beautifully maintained by Historic Scotland, well laid out with explanatory panels and signs. Approaching the monastic site, which lies in a protected hollow in the landscape, one first crosses the boundary wall or *vallum* which divided the sacred precincts of the monastery from the secular world beyond. Within this boundary were the early Christian chapel, probably sixth century, and various other monastic buildings and cells, of which only traces now remain. It is thought that St Blane was born on Bute in the sixth century, educated in Ireland and then returned to his native island to establish a monastery. The place-names of Strathblane and Dunblane show that he travelled further afield. There is also a Kilblane in Kintyre and a Kilblain near Dumfries. A 'hogback' tombstone outside the south door of the medieval chapel is sometimes pointed out as St Blane's grave, but this cannot be the case. This type of tombstone is now

well known from other examples in other places (eg, Luss) and is securely dated to the Viking period – centuries after St Blane's death.

The upper graveyard at St Blane's, reserved for the men of the parish

Continuing into the monastic precinct, the scene is dominated by the medieval chapel, dating from the twelfth century with later additions. Until the Reformation it came under the jurisdiction of Paisley Abbey, and was regularly used as a place of worship up to the beginning of the eighteenth century. The medieval graveyard is divided into two parts: the upper graveyard, nearest the chapel, was reserved for the men of the parish, while the lower graveyard, in which is situated the early Christian chapel, was reserved for the womenfolk. The medieval chapel is a beautiful little piece of architecture, with very worn dog-tooth decoration in the arch dividing the chancel from the nave.

This is a place for reflection and contemplation. Many visitors comment on the peaceful and almost magical atmosphere of St Blane's, and it is indeed very possible that it was a place of religious worship long before it was a Christian site. An unusual circular structure constructed of enormous stones, at some distance from the chapel but still within the boundary of the

The lower graveyard, where the women of the parish were buried

Opposite: The chapel interior

The 'Devil's Cauldron', possibly a prehistoric structure incorporated into the monastic complex at St Blane's

early monastery, has never been satisfactorily explained and it is quite likely that it is prehistoric, predating the monastic site. It is known as the 'Devil's Cauldron'.

There are many early Christian chapels on Bute, and many early Christian monasteries throughout Argyll and the isles, but there are few places in which so many of the elements that together make up the site are preserved so well. The date of its foundation is uncertain, but it is thought that it was there by AD574, only fifteen years after Columba arrived at Iona. It is thought that the monastery in the parish of Kingarth was independent of St Columba's ecclesiastical control, as the historian Bede notes that 'St Columba had no more jurisdiction in Lismore, than he had in Applecross or Kingarth'. The original monastery was probably destroyed in a Viking raid in 798.

Strangely, St Blane is not the patron saint of Bute – this honour is reserved for St Brendan. The reason for this is lost in the mists of antiquity, but the tradition is very old indeed. Yet, there are no dedications anywhere in Bute to St Brendan. The closest is across Kilbrannan Sound – the sound of Brendan – at the chapel beside Skipness Castle, in Kintyre. Natives of Bute are always known as 'Brandanes' – followers of Brendan. The earliest example of this usage is in John of Fordun's *Chronicle of the Scottish Nation*, in which 'John Stewart, with his Brendans' (in Latin, *Johannes Seneschallus, cum Brendanis*) fought with William Wallace against the English at the Battle of Falkirk in 1298. This was Sir John Stewart, the younger son of Alexander, the fourth High Steward. He and many of the men of Bute were killed at Falkirk in Wallace's last stand against Edward I of England. He and his men are buried in the old churchyard of Falkirk, where his grave and a memorial can be seen – erected, unsurprisingly, by the 3rd Marquess of Bute, renowned for his interest in Scottish history. In current usage, *both* of your parents must have been born on Bute before you can describe yourself as a 'Brandane'.

It is probable that the Brendan whom the men of Bute followed was St Brendan of Clonfert, Brendan the Navigator, whose voyages of exploration and adventure in a tiny curragh amongst the tempestuous seas of the North Atlantic have captured the imagination of seafarers everywhere and are brilliantly described in the medieval *Navigatio*, which has been described as the science fiction of its time. Brendan's voyages describe journeys up the west coasts of Scotland and Ireland, surviving the treacherous conditions and establishing churches as he went. The 3rd Marquess of Bute, something of an historian and scholar in his own right, came to the conclusion that Brendan's voyages could never have happened in reality, but in 1976 and 1977 Tim Severin and his crew proved otherwise, sailing a replica curragh up the coasts of Scotland and then on to Iceland and Greenland to the coasts of North America.

A distant view of the Iron Age hill-fort of Dunagoil, looking across to Arran

Returning from the time of St Blane to the twentieth century at the car park at the end of the public road, visitors may wish to travel still further back into history and visit the Iron Age vitrified fort on Dunagoil. The best access is from the lay-by just opposite Dunagoil Farm, from where it is an easy walk of about twenty minutes to the base of the fort. However, from here on it is a fair scramble to the summit and decidedly unsuitable for unsupervised children. There is a sheer drop on the seaward side, and indeed all around the fort except on the southern approaches.

Archaeological excavations at Dunagoil (Gaelic: *Dun-na-ghoil*, the fort of the stranger) were carried out in 1915, 1919 and 1925 and many of the finds are in the Bute Museum in Rothesay. Material found in a cave at the bottom of the cliff was found to date from both the Neolithic and the Bronze Age. A massive amount of Iron Age material was also recovered, including pottery, clay crucibles for casting bronze, a bloomery for smelting iron, bone and lignite objects and ornaments, spinning whorls, pieces of horse harness, lots of animal bones, stone whetstones and saddle querns (for grinding grain) and flint. There were also glass and enamel beads.

The Iron Age in Bute is thought to have started early in the first millennium BC, and a date of 850BC for the vitrified fort would fit in with what we know of comparable sites elsewhere. The fort is described as 'vitrified' because for long stretches of the summit wall the stones of the wall have melted as the result of tremendous heat, causing the rock to melt, bubble and create a glassy, enamelled appearance. At one time this was thought to be a construction technique, as the vitrified rock is incredibly hard and impregnable to attack, even with a modern pick. However, later research showed that the vitrified effect was due to the fact that the ramparts were timber-laced. When the buildings attached to these walls (on the inside) caught fire, either accidentally or as the result of enemy attack, the wall timbers would burn out in a high wind (not unusual in Bute!), causing a flue effect which could create the very high temperatures necessary to melt the rock – which has to have a high silica content to create the 'glassy' appearance. On sites where there is no silica in the local rock, walls would appear fire-cracked and reddened with the heat, but would not melt. There are few places anywhere in Scotland where the vitrified effect can be seen so clearly as at Dunagoil. There are also few forts so dangerous to visit, but with due care it is well worth the effort.

There are other archaeological sites in the nearby landscape. Excavations between 1958 and 1962 took place at the fort at Little Dunagoil, just south of Dunagoil Bay and showed traces of an Iron Age rampart, but also evidence of occupation from the Bronze Age until the thirteenth century. Again, many of the finds are in the Bute Museum. Accounts of the excavations were published in specialist archaeological journals, but summarised by Dorothy Marshall in her *History of Bute*.

Dunagoil Bay, at the south end of Bute

5 THE WEST SIDE

FROM THE CROSSROADS AT Kingarth, or returning from a visit to St Blane's, the road leading up the west side of Bute from Kingarth to Kilchattan Bay passes through fertile farmland. A string of farms provides a challenge in pronunciation for the visitor and an etymological puzzle for the place-name scholar. A welcome feature of recent years is the addition of large signs at each farm, on which their names are written in large, readable letters.

The first farm after the Kingarth crossroads is Langalchorad. To the Norse, a *gill* was a narrow glen watered by a stream, and the lang-gill or long, narrow glen of Kingarth seems to have been the glen beside Stravanan (Gaelic: *srath Mhanain*, Manan's or Magnus's strath). Just over a mile from Kingarth is the farm of Quochag (Gaelic: *caochag*, a mushroom). Next is Langelbuinoch (Gaelic: *buannachd*, profit), then Nether Stravanan and Kerrymenoch (Gaelic: *ceathramh meadhonach*, the middle quarter), followed by Gallachan (Gaelic: *gall achadh*, the stranger's field). Three miles from Kingarth is the turnoff for the west coast road, just before Loch Quien (Gaelic: *cuithean*, a little mound). There is a crannog, an Iron Age artificial island, on this loch.

The first farm after the turnoff is Ambrismore (Gaelic: *amar*, a channel or trough, and *mor*, big). A mile further on, is the farm of Scalpsie (Norse: *scalpr*, a small boat or 'shallop', and another *aig*, bay). In this case the farm takes its name from the bay of the same name. Now the road climbs up quite steeply, with a good view of Scalpsie Bay and the Iron Age dun (small fort) of Dun Scalpsie. The island of Inchmarnock comes into view, and it is worth stopping in the viewpoint provided at Mecknoch (Gaelic: *Beachdchnoc*, the view-hill) to read the information panels.

Now uninhabited, Inchmarnock, the island of St Marnoc, was once the home of a small farming community. Early in the nineteenth century the population was twenty-two, in three farms, at North Park, Mid Park and South Park, and the early Christian chapel, dedicated to St Marnoc for inspiration. Despite being less than forty miles from Glasgow and only half a mile from Bute across a sea channel, this was an exceedingly isolated community. For example, during the gales of the winter of 1971–2, the tenant of Mid Park was able to cross over to Bute only once during the month of November, twice during December and once in February. There was no

The jagged peaks of Arran, viewed from Ardscalpsie

telephone or mail service, and no pier or jetty. The island is only two and a half miles in length and half a mile wide.

Although life there in the end proved to be too tough for its human inhabitants, it is something of a paradise for the rest of nature. It is exceptionally rich in wild flowers, including scarlet pimpernel, campion, thrift, the rare oyster flower and a profusion of giant primroses. There are no trees but scrub birch, hazel and rowan grow well. Seals and basking sharks are common around its coasts. The bird life is also prolific, with an abundance of gulls, skuas, terns, curlews, pigeons, buzzards, peregrines, shags and ducks, including goosanders, mallards, teal and many others. There were corncrakes on the island in 1969. The colony of herring gulls is the largest in the Firth of Clyde – making the island not exactly a haven of peace and tranquillity!

A story in Adamnan's *Life of Columba* tells of the close relationship between Columba and Marnoc. In AD585 Columba was visiting the important monastery of Clonmacnois, whose abbot was determined to put on a good show for the visiting dignitary, by then an old man. Columba was protected from the elements by a canopy carried on poles by four bearers and the procession was proceeding with due solemnity when a small boy was discovered hiding underneath the folds of the canopy, clinging to the edge of Columba's cloak. As the lad was chastised and about to be sent packing, Columba intervened and asked for him to put out his tongue for inspection – not for medical reasons, but so that the saint could proclaim that this young boy's tongue was gifted by God with eloquence, and that he would grow up to become a saint of the church. This young lad was Marnoc, also known as Ernoc for reasons to do with the complications of Gaelic orthography. For example, Kilmarnock, the church of Marnoc, is in Gaelic *Cill mo Ern-oc*, so that the place-name Killearnan, in Ross-shire, is just as much associated with our saint as Inchmarnock in Bute or Dalmarnock in Glasgow. The root of his name is the Irish Gaelic *erna*, a whetstone, on which iron weapons are sharpened – an obvious metaphor for a saint's church-name.

That the island has had a long history was proved in 1961, when a jet necklace now in the Bute Museum was recovered from a Bronze Age cist burial. Fragments of ancient crosses have been found in and around the ruins of St Marnoc's chapel and are now also in the Bute Museum. At one time slates were quarried on Inchmarnock. In 1943 the island was evacuated by the government and used as a target for long-range gunfire.

The road now enters the lands of Kilmory, site of a chapel dedicated to Mary. Three Bronze Age cists were uncovered in 1933 at Little Kilmory and were found to contain the bones of children, aged seven, eleven and thirteen, according to the evidence of their teeth. An urn from this discovery is in the Bute Museum. The remains of a medieval castle can be seen beside

Scalpsie Bay, on the west coast of Bute

Kilmory Farm. Just past Kilmory is Kerryfearn (Gaelic: *ceathramh fearna*, alder tree quarter-land), after which the road turns inland past the farms of Quogach, sometimes spelled Cuagach or Cullach, (possibly Gaelic: *caol achadh*, lean or narrow field) and Kilwhinleck (possibly Gaelic: *cill cumhain leac*, the cell of the flat memorial stone of Conn, or perhaps St Cuimein, the seventh abbot of Iona).

At Milton two roads join at an acute angle, at a point less than two miles from Rothesay, but to return to the west coast it is necessary to turn sharply left, to the west, heading for the village of Straad (Gaelic: *sraid*, the street). Now just a few isolated houses, up to the end of the nineteenth century this was a self-contained community, in a distinctive part of the island. There was a busy harbour and a thriving little fleet of fishing boats, and a joiner, cooper, blacksmith, two cobblers and a miller served the little community – and there were two licensed inns in the neighbourhood.

The bay here is St Ninian's Bay, sweeping round to St Ninian's Point, on a narrow neck of land almost cut off at high tides. Here is another important early Christian site, dedicated to yet another important saint, though no others are as early or as important as Ninian. His main monastery was at Whithorn, on the Solway Firth, but he ranged far and wide. St Ninian's Isle, off Shetland, was the scene of an important find of Pictish ecclesiastical silver; the church at Drumnadrochit beside Loch Ness is also dedicated to Ninian; while MacCringan's Point, at the entrance to Campbeltown Loch, shows his presence there. The chapel on St Ninian's Point is very ruinous, but clear enough. On the neck of land leading to the Point are two small standing stones, protected by fencing. While not immediately impressive, their alignment may be what is important.

Returning to the crossroads at Ballianlay, we can pause to reflect on the difficulties of Gaelic place-names, and how cunningly their English versions can hide their true meanings, for this is undoubtedly *Baile-Fhionlaidh*, Finlay's township, where the rules of Gaelic orthography dictate that the 'F' is aspirated, rendering it silent and unpronounced. Now the road runs north for the last mile to the south end of Ettrick Bay, through the lands of Ardroscadale, a hybrid and tautological place-name containing the Gaelic *ard* and the Norse *ros*, both of which mean 'point', and the Norse *dalr*, a dale or fertile glen. In 1475 it was 'Ardrossigelle', so it is possible that the original Norse ending was *gill*, a defile or narrow glen. It is also possible that there is a Norse personal name hiding in the middle of this name, making it 'Rossi's glen'.

Before reaching Ettrick Bay the road passes the farm of Largievrechten. Returning towards Rothesay, we see the church of St Colmac ahead, and pass the farms of Cranslagvourity and Cranslagloan. These last two names were previously spelled as Kneslagvourarty (Gaelic: *Crioslach-Mhurachaidh*, Murdoch's border) and Kneslagloan (Gaelic: *Crioslacheanlaine*, the border of the bog or meadow). Largievrechten is Gaelic: *Learg-a-bhreachdain*, the slope covered with wheat.

KIPPERING

Near St Ninian's Point is a little building which is the remains of a kippering shed, where the commercial smoking of herring was first carried out. At one time nearly everybody in Straad and around St Ninian's Bay kept donkeys, which

were used to carry kippers or fresh fish across to Rothesay. In the New Statistical Account *for the parish of Rothesay (1840) it is said that: 'Large quantities of cockles are gathered at St Ninian's bay, and sent to Glasgow by a number of poor people, who thus make their living.'*

Opposite: The ruins of an early Christian chapel dedicated to St Ninian on St Ninian's Point, with the remains of a fish-processing shed in the background

71

6 THE CENTRAL BELT

Opposite and above: Loch Fad

THE CENTRAL VALLEY OF Bute, running from Rothesay south-west to Scalpsie Bay, is a part of the island likely to be traversed many times by visitors on their way to and from the many interesting attractions of the island. This is the famous Highland Boundary Fault, filled by Loch Fad (Gaelic: *fada*, long – the long loch) and Loch Quien. Loch Fad is the largest of Bute's freshwater lochs, two miles in length and a quarter of a mile wide.

The Highland Boundary Fault, or Highland Line, starts near Stonehaven on the north-east coast of Scotland in Aberdeenshire and proceeds south-west across the Scottish mainland, reaching the coast at Helensburgh, before surfacing again on Bute. To the north are igneous rocks and metamorphic Dalradian schists (550 million years old); to the south are sedimentary rocks – slates, Old Red Sandstone (360 million years old). The island's soils reflect the underlying geology. In the north the soil is acid, so the vegetation is of moorland type, with very few trees. The central belt has rich sandy soil, while the southern half of the island has predominantly the good, light loam typical of Old Red Sandstone landscapes.

Loch Fad was used as the water supply in the eighteenth century for Rothesay's developing linen industry, usually locally grown flax. A lade brought the water from Kirk Dam at the northern end of Loch Fad. The man who did the most to organise the water supply of Bute was Robert Thom of Greenock, a water engineer. He acquired the Rothesay mills, but realised that for the expansion he had in mind there was an inadequate water supply. During the 1820s he constructed a series of water cuts, nearly seven miles in all, in an elaborate system designed to carry water from Birgidale and Mount Stuart on the east and south-east, and from Scalpsie and Quien on the west, to a dam at Loch Fad. A series of aqueducts and bridges carried the water when needed and can still be seen in many parts of the island.

Thom was nothing if not ambitious, but he overstretched himself when he diverted the course of the Scoulag Burn and cut off the water supply to Mount Stuart, leading to a prolonged legal battle with the Marquess of Bute. Thom's skill in surveying was outstanding – and bear in mind that the first Ordnance Survey maps of Bute were not published until the 1860s, fifty years after he started his works.

The Rothesay cotton mills were of vital importance to the town's economy during the nineteenth century. In 1801 there were 700 cotton workers and 200 weavers, including children who worked in the mills from 6am until 7pm, and by the 1820s the cotton industry was employing well over 1,000 workers. By 1840 one mill alone employed over 350 people. After 1860 the industry declined and by 1872 there were only 600 workers in the industry. By 1882 the peak of five mills was reduced to one. Various reasons have been offered for the decline of the Bute mills. The introduction of steam power required the use of heavy machinery unsuitable for the Rothesay mills, but geographical factors and changing patterns of transport and distribution were perhaps just as important. Workers left the island to work in mainland mills, mainly in Lanarkshire, causing a decline in the island's population.

The lands of Birgidale (Norse: *borgr-dalr*, fort-valley), overlooking Loch Fad from the south, are further evidence of Norse presence on Bute. Another farm in the central valley is Kerrycrusach (Gaelic: *ceathramh*, a quarter-land, and *croiseag*, a little cross), probably meaning 'the district of the little crosses' – Crossbeg and Crossmore are both places in the immediate vicinity.

WILDLIFE ON LOCH FAD

Loch Fad is an important refuge for birds and wildfowl, and a Central Lochs of Bute Site of Special Scientific Interest (SSSI) has been created for their protection. Fishing on Loch Fad is carefully controlled.

The loch is well stocked with rainbow and brown trout, with thirty boats available for hire and bank angling available from the Isle of Bute Trout Company Limited (tel: 01700 504871). There are also pike in Loch Fad. A bird hide has been provided overlooking Kirk Dam at the north end of the loch, where there is a very rich variety of wildfowl within walking distance of Rothesay. Disabled access is provided, along with fencing to keep out livestock on the stretch of land adjacent to the Causeway between the Dam and Loch Fad.

7 MOUNT STUART

Previous pages and above: Mount Stuart, the palatial home of the Bute family, now open to the public

Opposite: Ferns in the Pavilion at Mount Stuart

OPENED TO THE PUBLIC for the first time in 1995, this wonderfully excessive Victorian Gothic mansion is now seen to be one of Scotland's most spectacular stately homes. Already attracting over 30,000 visitors a year (1997), it has helped to fill the vacuum created in Bute with the decline of traditional tourism, and has opened up new possibilities for the management and development of tourism on the island.

Mount Stuart is the architectural fantasy of the 3rd Marquess of Bute (1847–1900) and his architect Sir Robert Rowand Anderson. It sits in 300 acres (120ha) of designed landscape, which is also open to the public. The present house is the second Mount Stuart house on the site – the original house was built in 1719 but burned down in 1877. Designs were prepared and construction of the replacement began in 1880. By 1886 it was ready for occupation and was justly described at the time as 'palatial'. No expense was spared: a swimming bath was the first heated pool to be installed in any house and Mount Stuart was the first house in Scotland to be lit by electricity.

The man of whom it was said that he 'had of course no occasion to consider the question of expense' was John Patrick Crichton-Stuart, 3rd Marquess of Bute. When he came of age in 1868 it was said that he had an annual income of £300,000 and was the richest man in Britain. Where did this vast wealth come from and how did this family achieve the heights of unimaginable fame and fortune?

The current family of Crichton-Stuart has its origins in the time of David I, when their ancestor Walter Fitz Alan became his Seneschal or Steward. From 1157 the post of Steward became hereditary and from this time dates the Stewart or Stuart surname. The 'Crichton' element was only added to the Bute family's name by the 2nd Marquess of Bute in 1805 when his mother Penelope Crichton was the heiress of the 6th Earl of Dumfries.

Inside the Pavilion at Mount Stuart

Opposite: The Rock Garden in the grounds of Mount Stuart

By 1204, the hereditary Stewards or Stuarts held lands in Bute. One of their descendants, Walter, married the daughter of Robert the Bruce in 1315; their son became Robert II, the first Stewart king. Subsequently, the lineage gets decidedly murky. A John Stuart was appointed hereditary Sheriff of Bute in 1385, but his relationship to his royal ancestor is unclear. Robert II married twice and had thirteen legitimate children but at least another eight born out of wedlock, and it is not too clear exactly which of all these children is the ancestor of the Stuarts of Bute. However, the family continued to prosper and in 1498 James IV rewarded their loyalty with the additional hereditary titles of Captain and Keeper of Rothesay Castle.

The family moved out of the castle and into the nearby Old Mansion House on the High Street in Rothesay after the destruction of the castle by the army of the 9th Earl of Argyll in 1685. Sir James Stewart, 3rd Baronet, was created Earl of Bute in 1703: among his other titles were Viscount Kingarth and Lord Mount Stuart – the first use of that name. Plans for the first Mount Stuart House were drawn up by the 2nd Earl in 1716, with the house completed by 1719.

The family hit the national stage in the time of the 3rd Earl, John Stuart (1713–1792). A personal adviser and confidant of George III, he was made a Knight of the Garter in 1762 and was Prime Minister in 1762–3. A failure as a politician, he was a great patron of the arts and a great collector of paintings and fine furnishings, many of which are in Mount Stuart today. He had a home in Bedfordshire, Luton Park, redesigned by Robert Adam to house his collections. He had another home in Hampshire, Highcliffe House, which was also furnished lavishly.

As befits a Prime Minister of Great Britain, Lord Bute has a long entry in the *Dictionary of National Biography*, but unfortunately, although it gives a very full description of his life and work, it is far from flattering:

Bute was a proud but well-intentioned nobleman, with a handsome person and pompous manners. He possessed some talent for intrigue, but his abilities were meagre, and his disposition irresolute. Though admirably qualified to manage the petty details of a little court, he was utterly unfit to direct the destinies of a great nation. He had no knowledge of public business, no experience of parliamentary debate, no skill either in the management of men or in the administration of affairs . . . The details of his administration are peculiarly disgraceful, and for corruption and financial incapacity it is not likely to be surpassed.

However, the 3rd Earl of Bute was not without redeeming features and indeed it has been suggested that the *DNB* entry above reiterates the prejudices of his political opponents. He was a distinguished botanist and was involved in the creation of Kew Gardens. In 1780 he became the first President of the Society of Antiquaries of Scotland. It is thought that both Dr Samuel Johnson and Robert Adam benefited from his patronage, as well as Allan Ramsay, Sir Joshua Reynolds and Thomas Gainsborough. He had five sons and six daughters.

His son, the 4th Earl of Bute, married well, not once but twice, and was moreover created Marquess of Bute in 1796. His first wife, to whom he was married in 1766, was the daughter of Viscount Windsor and Baron Mountjoy, who later inherited vast estates and wealth in Cardiff and South Wales; his second wife was another heiress, the daughter of Thomas Coutts, the banker.

In 1814 the 1st Marquess was succeeded by his grandson – his son had predeceased him. The 2nd Marquess of Bute (1793–1848) consolidated his family's position and made further fortunes from the development of his Welsh estates – it was he who built Cardiff Docks, turning that city into a major seaport.

When the 2nd Marquess died in 1848, his son, who would not 'come of age' until 1868, was only six months old. During his long minority his trustees applied themselves to the problem of the family finances. His father had expanded his properties and invested well, but still had enormous debts. It is reckoned that he had combined mortgages and business debts of £493,887; the interest on his huge loans and mortgages, usually 4 per cent, was paid out of annual estate income. In the twenty-one years following the death of the 2nd Marquess, the trustees applied all the estate income to clear the debts. The young heir was an orphan from the age of eleven, and without expensive adult dependants to maintain, the trustees were able to launch him into adult life clear of all debts, with a massive annual income and with lucrative investment income to come.

And so to the 3rd Marquess, John Patrick Crichton-Stuart, reputedly the richest man in Britain (1847–1900). He was a Victorian polymath, a man of wide interests, in archaeology, history, astrology and religion, a great patron of the arts, a romantic and mystic. He shocked Victorian society by converting to Catholicism in 1868 – how different Mount Stuart would have been if he had followed the more austere architectural tastes of his Protestant Scottish contemporaries. In South Wales, the 3rd Marquess began to indulge his fantasies, first at Cardiff Castle, and then at the extravagantly lavish Castell Coch. In Scotland, he sponsored about sixty building projects and was patron to a dozen architects. Among the buildings which benefited from his patronage were Falkland Palace, Pluscarden Priory and Dunblane Cathedral. The Bute Hall at the University of Glasgow, built in 1882, was the gift of the 3rd Marquess – many readers may have sat exams there, and hopefully nearly as many will have attended graduation ceremonies there.

Statue of Augusta, mother of George III, in the grounds of Mount Stuart

How ironic then that the 3rd Marquess's own home on Bute was largely destroyed by fire on 3 December 1877. The north and south wings survived, but the central core of the old Mount Stuart was burnt out. He hired Scotland's leading exponent of Victorian Gothic, Sir Robert Rowand Anderson and assembled a workforce of craftsmen, including many who had worked on his projects in Wales, to carry his dreams and fantasies through to reality. The project was uncompleted at his death in 1900. The incredible chapel, begun in 1896, was not finally completed until 1998.

In the *Dictionary of National Biography*, the 3rd Marquess's life and career is detailed in most favourable terms, despite the 'profound sensation' of his conversion to Catholicism. There is a striking description of his physical appearance: 'In stature Bute was fully six feet. He was proportionately broad, with square shoulders, handsome, with distinguished bearing, dark brown hair and beard, blue grey eyes, and high-bridged nose.'

John, the 4th Marquess (1881–1947) carried the works at Mount Stuart forward, though his own tastes were more modest, or at least more Classical than Gothic. Like his predecessors, he was a great patron of architecture. In 1941 he became the first chairman of the Scottish National Buildings Record, now the National Monuments Record of Scotland.

His son John, the 5th Marquess (1907–1956), held the title for only nine years before he was succeeded in his turn by his son John. He is remembered for presenting Cardiff Castle to the city of Cardiff, shortly after his father's death in 1947. John, the 6th Marquess of Bute (1933–1993) was also greatly interested in Scotland's architectural heritage, serving as both the chairman of the National Trust for Scotland and the Historic Buildings Council for Scotland. Johnny Dumfries, as he is always known, the son of the 6th Marquess and a former Formula One racing driver, is the chairman of the Mount Stuart Trust, which undertook to complete the chapel, maintain the building and grounds, and open it to the public. Since succeeding as the 7th Marquess of Bute, Johnny Dumfries has brought a definite air of change and openness to the running of the estate, which is greatly to be welcomed.

The Mount Stuart Trust has published a small but lavishly illustrated guidebook to the house and gardens, with details of how the house was built, and its interior design. The Marble Hall, the Dining Room, the Entrance Hall, the Horoscope Room, the Conservatory, the Henry VIII Bedroom (so-called from a portrait which hangs there), the Drawing Room and the Chapel almost defy description, and we can only look forward in due course to fuller publications. Now that the public's appetite has been whetted, not to mention that of Scotland's architectural historians who must be having a field day, further tomes which celebrate the riches of this Gothic palace are surely required. A visit to Mount Stuart is thoroughly recommended. Day visitors from Glasgow and central Scotland can buy through-travel tickets which include train, ferry and bus transport to the house and gardens, as well as the price of admission. Entry to Mount Stuart is by the turnoff just past Kerrycroy; car parks and catering facilities are provided.

The gardens are also briefly described in the Mount Stuart booklet, and also in a more useful folding leaflet which contains a map of the grounds, or 'policies', as they are known in Scotland. Dating from 1717, the grounds are extensive but well looked after, with a good network of footpaths and plenty of opportunities for picnics. Of several buildings and constructions throughout the gardens, the most unusual is perhaps the column surmounted by a statue – not of one of the Earls or Marquesses of Bute, but in honour of Augusta, the mother of George III, to whom the 3rd Earl was apparently devoted. It was originally raised in the grounds of Luton Park. The Latin inscription on the pedestal is from Virgil's Aeneid, and is translated as: 'So long as I am conscious and my spirit controls my limbs' – with the unexpressed sentiment that, as long as these conditions persist, 'you will remain in my memory'.

The Wee Garden, Mount Stuart

8 EARLY VISITORS TO BUTE

DEAN MONRO

Donald Monro was Archdeacon of the Isles before the Reformation, and subsequently became one of the leading scholars of the Reformed Church of Scotland. His manuscript account of more than 40 Scottish islands, written in 1549, throws much light on the history, topography and place-names of the Hebrides, with a wealth of detail on the way of life of ordinary people.

Monro was born about the beginning of the sixteenth century, and was related to several of the most influential families in the Highlands and Islands of Scotland. His own family came from Easter Ross. He describes himself as 'High Dean of the Islands', from the Latin 'archidiaconus Insularum'. He died around 1575.

Opposite: St Ninian's Bay, on the west side of Bute

FROM VERY EARLY TIMES, visitors commented on Bute's distinctive features, and it is interesting to see what was said about the island and its attractions in the past. In Dean Monro's *Description of the Western Isles of Scotland* (1549), Bute is described as having:

> very fertyle ground, namelie for aitts [oats], with two strengthes [fortresses]; the ane is the round castle of Buitt, callit Rosay of the auld, and Borrowstone [burgh-town] about it callit Buitt. Before the town ane castle is ane bay of sea, quhilk [which] is a gude heavin [haven] for ships to ly upon ankers.

This account encompasses the important features of Bute – its fertility, its unusual round castle, its royal burgh, and the anchorage of Rothesay Bay, much in demand by the Royal Navy during World War II. Monro goes on to describe Bute's other 'strengthe':

> That uther castle is callit the castle of Kames, quhilk Kames in Erishe [Irish, ie Gaelic] is, alsmeikle as to say, in English the bay castle.

This is interesting as an early attempt at toponymy, the study of place-names, as Monro notes that 'Kames' is derived from the Gaelic *camus*, meaning 'bay'. He now turns from the castles to the churches:

> In this ile there is twa paroche [parish] kirks, that ane southe callit the Kirk of Bride, the uther northe in the Borrowstone of Buitt, with twa chappells, ane of them above the town of Buitt [ie, Rothesay, in Gaelic *Baille Bhoid*], the uther under the forsaid castle of Kames.

Monro also has a brief description of Inchmarnock – 'Inche Mernoche' – which clearly, at the end of the sixteenth century, was a thriving community, well cultivated, despite its small extent:

> On the west southwest of it [Bute] lyes ane little iyle callit Inch Mernocke, twa myle fra sea, low mayne ground, weill inhabit and manurit, ane myle lange and half myle breadthe.

In an atlas published in Amsterdam in 1654, there is another record of an early visitor to Bute – albeit a rather indirect one. The decorative and colourful printed map published by the Blaeu firm of cartographers in 1654 is based on a manuscript survey, now lost, by Timothy Pont, a native of Caithness. After graduating from St Andrew's University in the early 1580s, he spent ten years, from 1585 to 1595, walking around the whole of

Scotland, including the islands, with a view to compiling an atlas of Scotland to rival Saxton's *Atlas of England and Wales*, published in 1579. A letter of 1648 from Robert Gordon to Sir John Scot of Scotstarvet, printed in the 1654 atlas, gives some idea of Timothy Pont's achievement:

. . . with small means and no favouring patron, he undertook the whole of this task forty years ago: he travelled on foot right through the whole of this kingdom, as no one before him had done; he visited all the islands, occupied for the most part by inhabitants hostile and uncivilised, and with a language different from our own; being often stripped, as he told me, by the fierce robbers, and suffering not seldom all the hardships of the dangerous journey, nevertheless at no time was he overcome by the difficulties, nor was he disheartened.

Pont died around 1613, still a comparatively young man, so never saw his project brought to fruition. We can only hope that he was well treated by the inhabitants of Bute, despite the fact that they spoke a strange language. Certainly the map of Bute, published in the Blaeu atlas of 1654 and based on Pont's survey, gives the impression that he covered the whole island from top to bottom, from *Row* (Rhubodach) to *Kilblain*, *Suychattan* (Suidhe Chattan) and *Doun ouil* (Dunagoil).

The main features of the island of 'Boot' are represented, though he places the island of Inchmarnock (*Mernoch*) much too far north, at the mouth of Ettrick Bay. The central valley of Bute, with *Loch Fad* and *Scaplie Loch* (Loch Quien), is accurately shown, with a range of hills to the north of the lochs giving a good visual impression of a long, straight cut across the island. As is often the case with Pont's Gaelic place-names, they are written phonetically, as he heard them pronounced on Bute, and this is often helpful to us in deciphering corrupted and anglicised names. Thus, St Colmac is *Kilmachalmak* and Ascog is *Ascock*. Bute's *kil*- names are all there, along with *Wester Kems Cast.* – the castle of Wester Kames. There is a castle shown on *Castel oilen Greg*, a little turret with a banner flying

proudly in the breeze, on a tiny islet in *The Kyles*, right at the north end of Bute. It is interesting that Rothesay is shown as an island in Rothesay Bay, with narrow channels of water surrounding it – perhaps the Amsterdam engraver's attempt to depict Pont's Rothesay Castle, with its moat. It is an important map – an interesting record of human settlement on Bute at the end of the sixteenth century.

A hundred years later, in his *Description of the Western Islands of Scotland* (1703), Martin Martin, himself a native of the Isle of Skye and a Gaelic speaker, gives a reasonable description of the natural environment of 'The Isle of Boot':

> The north end of this isle is mountainous and heathy, being more designed for pasturage than cultivation; the mold [soil] is brown or black, and in some parts clayie; the ground yields a good produce of oats, barley, and pease; there is but little wood growing there, yet there is a coppice at the side of Loch Fad. The ground is arable from the middle to the southward.

Martin has some very observant detail about the burgh of Rothesay and its castle:

The Royal Chapel within Rothesay Castle

Overleaf: Columnar basalt on the cliffs of Dunagoil

87

This town is a very ancient royal burgh, but thinly peopled, there not being above a hundred families in it, and they have no foreign trade. On the north side of Rothesay there is a very ancient ruinous fort, round in form, having a thick wall; it is surrounded with a wet ditch; it has a gate on the south, and a double gate on the east, and a bastion on each side the gate, and without these there's a draw-bridge, and the sea flows within forty yards of it. The fort is large enough for exercising a battallion of men; it has a chappel, and several little houses within; and a large house of four stories high, fronting the eastern gate.

It is interesting to note that the castle is now much further than forty yards from the sea, due to the reclamation of land on the sea-front, esplanade and harbour in the nineteenth century. Martin Martin goes on to make some observations about the people living on Bute at the beginning of the eighteenth century:

> All the inhabitants are Protestants… The natives here are not troubled with any epidemical disease. The small pox visits them commonly once every sixth or seventh year… The inhabitants generally speak the English and Irish tongue, and wear the same habit with those of the other islands. They are very industrious fishers, especially for herring, for which use they are furnished with about 80 large boats. The tenants pay their rents with the profit of herrings. They are to be had anywhere on the western coast.

Another important record of an early visit to Bute is Thomas Pennant's account in his *Voyage to the Hebrides* (1769). He devotes seven pages of his book to Bute, and has an important engraving of Rothesay Castle as a roofless ruin, with the Mercat Cross and some of the town's buildings in the background. Pennant, from Wales himself, arrived on Bute at 'Mount Stewart':

> …a modern house with a handsome front and wings: the situation very fine, in an eminence in the midst of a wood, where trees grow with as much vigour as in the more Southern parts, and extend far beneath on each side; and Throstles, and other birds of song, fill the groves with their melody.

Pennant had obviously succumbed to the magic of Bute, as visitors still do. He comments on the enclosing hedges – 'tall, thick and vigorous'. The main produce of the island was barley, oats and potatoes, with turnips recently introduced successfully. Cattle and sheep were reared

Farmland near Dunagoil, at the south end of Bute

A WELSH TOURIST

Thomas Pennant was born at Downing, Flintshire, in 1726. Throughout the eighteenth century he wrote books on natural history, with an interest in ornithology, minerals and fossils. In 1771 were published first his Synopsis of quadrupeds, *followed later in the year by his first travel book* A tour of Scotland in 1769. *This was so successful that in 1774 he published two more volumes of his travels in Scotland, including the islands. In later years he wrote of his travels and adventures in Wales, described his ascent of Snowdon, and in 1782 published his* Journey from Chester to London. *These books did much to encourage travel and tourism among his literary contemporaries, including Boswell and Johnson. He died at his family home in 1798.*

on all the farms. As with many later visitors, Pennant comments on Bute's mild climate:

> The air is in general temperate: no mists or thick rolling fogs from the sea, called in the North, a *harle*, ever infest this island. Snow is scarcely ever known to be here; and even that of last winter, so remarkable for its depth and duration in other places, was in this island scarce two inches deep. The evils of this place are winds and rains, the last coming in deluges from the West.

This last sentence smacks of personal experience, though Bute is not as wet as the neighbouring areas of Arran and Cowal.

On 18 June 1772, Pennant rode to 'the hill of *Kil-Chattan*, a round eminence, from whence is a vast view of all around, insular and mainland.' He visited St Blane's church – 'the ruin of old *Kin-garth* church', where he notes the tradition of the upper and lower burial grounds for the men and women of the parish, and also 'a circular inclosure called the *Devil's Cauldron*'.

Rothesay is described by Pennant as 'a small but well-built town of small houses, and about two hundred families'. The history of Rothesay Castle is told in some detail, quoting from older historians – Buchanan, Boethius and John Major.

Pennant notes that because St Brendan had once built a cell on Bute and used it as a retreat, 'the natives of the isle, and also of Arran, have been sometimes styled *Brandani* – Brandanes'. He also briefly mentions 'Inch-Marnoc', with a hundred and twenty acres of arable land, forty acres of brush wood, three hundred acres of moor, and 'vast strata of coral and shells on the West side'.

In the *Old Statistical Account* (1791), the Reverend Mr James Thorburn gives some very interesting accounts of the Parish of Kingarth and the way of life of the people at the end of the eighteenth century. By his time, the landscape had been enclosed – 'nearly the whole of the parish is inclosed and subdivided with ditch and hedge, which afford shelter and warmth, and make an agreeable appearance'. It is still the case that the hedges of Bute are unusual in a west coast island and are often commented upon. Thorburn noted that the main crops were 'barley, turnip, rye-grass and clover of every kind'. The barley was sold on the island, for the distilling of whisky; oats were taken to the nearest market town, Largs, across the Clyde on the mainland. For most of the year the people lived on potatoes and herrings. The crops were harvested by women – though the men did help out: 'There are no men-reapers; the corn is all cut down by women; and the men tie the sheaves and stook them.' Mr Thorburn had been long enough on Bute to come to terms with the climate – both its good points and its bad points:

This parish, though damp, is mild and temperate, and very healthy, owing probably to the saline particles impregnating the air, and the dry sandy soil of the parish. There are no epidemical diseases in the parish. The only distemper is the rheumatism; but it is not frequent. There are many instances of longevity in the parish. Three men died this winter, one 94, each of the other two 84 years old.

So, no mention of smallpox, a century after Martin Martin's visit. Thorburn makes some comments about the 'Language and Character' of the people, criticising the use of Gaelic as a hindrance to progress:

Most of the natives speak English very well; although, in conversing with one another, they seem to be fond of the Gaelic, their mother tongue, which chiefly prevails among the old people, and may have been an hindrance to the more easy and more ready introduction of new methods of improvements in the parish. They are a sober, peaceable, and charitable people.

Thorburn found that there were two main disadvantages to living on Bute. One was the price of coal, all of which had to be imported. The second involved a criticism of the local farmers:

The farmers being employed the most part of the summer in casting and leading peats, cannot provide manure for their farms ... the greatest disadvantage to the farming interest of the parish is the bounty to the buss-fishing, which is carried on to a great extent in Rothesay. Few farmer's sons are bred to farming. To purchase a small share in a herring buss, and become master of it, seems to be their great ambition.

Mr Thorburn's opposite number in the parish of Rothesay was the Reverend Mr Archibald McLea, who in his contribution to the *Old Statistical Account* gives a very detailed analysis of the population of Rothesay, based on annual figures from 1766 to 1790, during which time the population rose from 1,158 to 2,607. It is clear that in the last half of the eighteenth century there were a lot of changes in the town:

There is no particular account of the antient state of the population of the parish; but, from the number of ruinous and waste houses which were in the town of Rothesay, it would appear to have been pretty populous, and of some note at an early period. About the year 1762, some of these ruins were begun to be rebuilt; and, since that period, the town has been gradually increasing so much, that, not only the former ruinous houses have been all re-built, but a number of new streets laid out and finished.

STATISTICAL ACCOUNTS

Each of the parishes of Bute is covered in each of the three Statistical Accounts, providing a snapshot of life on the island in the 1790s, the 1840s and the 1960s.

These parish surveys, although amounting to only a few pages, give a wealth of detail and a tremendous insight into the life and customs of the local people. As well as providing statistical information on population, exports and imports, crop yields and local industries, there is a description of the topography of the parish, the more important antiquities and castles, an account of the climate and some detail of important local families.

Overleaf: The Serpentine, winding its way up the hill above the town, viewed from Rothesay Castle

Gaelic Language

At the time of the 1991 Census, there were 65,000 Gaelic speakers in Scotland, out of a total population of 4,962,152. Even including learners, less than 2 per cent of Scots can speak Gaelic, and all of these are bilingual.

At the 1981 Census, there were 27,000 people from Eire resident in Scotland, and 33,000 from Asia, and the largest group of non-Scots living in Scotland were in fact English-born – 297,784, or 5.7 per cent. While there is a concentration of Gaelic speakers in the Western Isles and Skye, it is still the case that over half of all Gaelic speakers live in other parts of Scotland, outside the current Gaelic heartland.

It is reckoned that, in 1600, Scotland's population was about 800,000, growing to around one million by the time of the Treaty of Union in 1707.

The Gaelic language was introduced into what later became the Kingdom of Scotland in the sixth century, from Ireland, and by the late Middle Ages had spread throughout most of Scotland north of the Forth–Clyde isthmus, as well as into Galloway in the south-west.

The spread of Gaelic is illustrated most graphically by the study of Gaelic place-names, which still exists in parts of the country where the language has not been spoken for centuries. Current developments in Gaelic culture allow for modest optimism that the language will survive.

Mr McLea thought that the reason for the increase in population was the establishment of a custom house in Rothesay in 1766, which increased trade and growth of the herring fishery, and the appearance of a cotton spinning mill in the 1770s. Like Mr Thorburn, he complains about the price of coal and notes that for the islanders the only available fuel was peat. He confirms the attraction of herring fishing to the young men of Bute and gives a satisfactory report on the character of the population: 'the people enjoy, in a considerable degree, the comforts and advantages of society, and seem contented with their situation and circumstances'.

By the time of the *New Statistical Account* in the 1840s, there had been some changes on the island. The minister of the parish of Kingarth, writing in June 1840, was the Reverend John Buchanan, whose comments on St Blane's we have already noted. His description of the parish is very full and detailed, and an excellent source of information on the social history of Bute. His remarks on the character of the population are as revealing of Mr Buchanan as of his subjects:

> The English language is that spoken in general by the inhabitants. Persons who have come to maturity understand commonly the Gaelic language also; but its use has much decreased within the last forty years, and is now chiefly confined to the aged, among the natives of the parish. The people are cultivated in their habits. They are, for the most part, remarkable for cleanliness both in their persons and in their dwellings. Their dress is plain and decent. The food of the peasantry equals, in plenty and quality, that of any of their degree in the country. All classes enjoy a full ordinary share of the comforts and advantages belonging to their situation in life, and appear to be correspondingly contented and happy. In their intellectual, moral and religious character, they afford a fair specimen of their countrymen. Smuggling is wholly unknown among them; and in no similar district, probably, is there less of poaching.

Mr Buchanan complains about the lack of a post office at the south end of the island in his parish, but praises the internal communications – the roads and bridges being excellent. He mentions that there are three schools in the parish, and that everybody over the age of fifteen can read and write. There is one respect, however, in which he worries about the morals of his parishioners:

> There are six ale-houses in the parish; three of which are in the village of Kilchatan-bay. Of these last, two are superfluous, and likely to prove injurious to morals, as the multiplication of such houses, especially in villages, is invariably found to be.

There had been a change of diet since the 1790s. Whereas the population were living then on potatoes and herring for three-quarters of the year, by 1840 herring 'have ceased to be . . . an important article of subsistence. Animal food has become general; and it has become common for cottagers to rear pigs and poultry for their own use'. There had also been a change, by 1840, in the aspirations of farmers' sons, who are no longer lured away to the fishing boats of Rothesay but are eager to stay on the farm – only fifteen of them are working in the herring fishery.

For the parish of Rothesay, the Reverend Robert Craig gives a full account of the burgh and landward sections of the parish, in his contribution to the *New Statistical Account* (1840). He uses data collected by one of the cotton mills to compile detailed tables of temperature, wind direction and rainfall in Rothesay and makes some general observations on the climate.

Mr Craig also has some interesting observations on the beginnings of Rothesay's appeal to what we would call the tourist trade:

> For many years Rothesay was resorted to by such sea bathers as were fond of retirement, but the introduction of steam navigation in 1814 having rendered access to this place so easy, it has now become a fashionable watering-place. The demand for houses has increased so much on this account, that now new streets have been laid off on each side of the bay, and additional houses are constantly erecting.

This tourist boom was to continue for the rest of the nineteenth century, and did not start to diminish alarmingly until after World War II – we have already commented on the way in which the growth of Mediterranean packaged tourism was the death knell of the 'Costa Clyde'.

On the character and habits of the people, Mr Craig's comments are similar to those of his colleague in Kingarth:

> The English language is generally spoken by the natives, and the Gaelic has rapidly fallen into disuse during the last forty years. Scarcely any of the children now learn or understand it.

This attitude to Gaelic we view with horror today, but for many years it was the stated policy of the education authorities in Gaelic-speaking areas that the language of state education should be English only – and in many schools pupils were punished, even beaten, if they were caught speaking Gaelic to each other in the playground. In its goal of eradicating Gaelic as the language of the ordinary people of the Highlands and Islands, this policy was largely successful, so that today there can be only a handful of the very oldest people who speak only Gaelic, and almost everybody who is a native speaker of Gaelic can read and write in English too. In recent years the Gaelic language has staged something of a revival, but it is still in dire straits. At the most optimistic estimate, only 1 per cent of the population of Scotland are fluent in Gaelic.

OLD STATISTICAL ACCOUNT

Sir John Sinclair of Ulbster (1754–1835) conceived the idea of a survey of all the parishes of Scotland, published in 20 volumes from 1791–8 as Statistical Account of Scotland. *Each parish minister prepared an account of their parish to a standard format, which was then edited by Sinclair. It is an unrivalled and essential source for the social history of Scotland at the end of the eighteenth century, poised on the edge of great changes.*

Born in Thurso Castle, Sinclair was educated at Edinburgh High School and the universities of Edinburgh, Glasgow and Oxford. He was called to the bar in both Scotland and England and inherited considerable properties in Caithness, for which he was MP from 1780–1811. His speciality, on which he wrote extensively, was the agricultural improvement of his native land.

In the 1840s Sinclair's parish surveys were brought up to date in the New Statistical Account of Scotland; *in the 1960s a* Third Statistical Account of Scotland *was started, and recently completed.*

As to the standards of public cleanliness and hygiene, Mr Craig was quite complimentary:

> The habits of the people in regard to cleanliness and comfort are constantly improving. This is owing partly to all the new houses being of a better construction than formerly, partly to the influence of free communication with other places, and partly to prizes which were awarded by a Society, to those who had the cleanest cottages, in the country part of the parish.

In their dress, the people of Bute wore what ordinary people wore anywhere in the Lowlands; their diet in 1840, in Rothesay, was still oatmeal and potatoes, with herrings and salt beef in winter, and wheat bread – there were eight master bakers in Rothesay. Summarising the state of his parishioners, Mr Craig states:

> The population generally enjoy much comfort, and many advantages for improvement. They are remarkably contented, orderly, and peaceable, and are distinguished for their sobriety and attention to the observances of religion. Poaching and smuggling are nearly unknown.

Mr Craig's only real criticism involved, inevitably, the question of strong drink:

> There are in the parish 51 houses licensed to sell spirits, and 4 to sell porter and ale alone. The number of them is unquestionably injurious to public morals, as it tends to lower the character of the houses themselves; and multiplies the allurements to drinking and excess.

Communications with the outside world improved immeasurably after the introduction of steam ships. There were two posts a day from Glasgow and Greenock, with one on Sunday – which the minister thought completely wrong, 'being both a profanation of the day, and quite unnecessary for business'. By 1840 there were seven vessels sailing to and from Glasgow, at a time when 19,000 barrels of salt herring were sent to market and 6,000 tons of coals imported. The first steamer reached Rothesay in 1814; its average speed being six miles an hour according to Mr Craig.

9 WITCHCRAFT IN BUTE

PRESERVED IN THE CHARTER Room at Inveraray is a manuscript volume recording matters connected with charges of witchcraft in Rothesay in 1662. It has no title, and the author cannot be identified. In 1920 the Scottish History Society published the material, or as much of it as the editor could decipher, in the first twenty-seven of their *Highland Papers*, volume 3. It consists of a series of statements taken from women who were suspected of being involved in witchcraft or 'charming', and statements taken from a number of local worthies – ministers, merchants and town officials.

To our late-twentieth-century sensitivities the atmosphere of superstition and ignorance seems incredible, but a cursory perusal of our tabloid press should warn against smugness and complacency in these matters. Some of the circumstances described as suspicious we would discount as mere coincidence, but underlying the mood of fear and persecution there is a layer of reality in which some women do seem to have been involved in strange rituals and bizarre behaviours. The documents, as well as shedding light on a dark corner of our social history, are an interesting record of real people and real places, in Bute in 1662.

Some of the stories hint at genuine fear of the suspected witches throughout the community. For example, there are several accounts of these women appearing in dreams. One of the women under suspicion was Jonet (Janet) Morisone (various spellings of her name appear). On 16 January 1662, Robert Stewart declared that about two years ago Nans (Nancy?) Mitchell 'dreamt about Jonet Morison in her bed in the night'. She woke, frightened at her dream, only to find that her young child was trembling from 'a very unnaturall lyke disease' of which he died. On 28 February, Jonet Boyd declared that about a year and a half before, while breastfeeding an infant, and with 'abundance of milk', she dreamed one night that she was attacked by Katherine Moore who 'took a great nipp out of her pape'. On waking from the dream, Jonet Boyd found that her milk supply had dried up, 'and that the place quhair [where] she dreamed that the said Katherine nipped her was blue'. In another case, Margrat MacWilliam was suspected of causing the milk supply of Major Ramsey's cows to dry up: 'his ky gert no milk'. He went to confront the suspect: 'he cam to her and upbradded her and said to her give my ky there milk agane or I'll burn thee myselfe'. When the Major arrived home he found that 'upon his returne the ky gave their milk'.

ATTITUDES TO WITCHCRAFT

In Scotland, trials for witchcraft, accompanied by torture, were very frequent in the seventeenth century. The last trial and execution in Scotland was in 1722. James IV of Scotland believed implicitly in witches and their ability to inflict 'spells' of weather at times of national crisis.

The attitude of the church to witchcraft before the more enlightened attitudes of the eighteenth century rests on three main factors: the Biblical recognition of its reality, the universal belief in demons and magic, and the identification of these demons with heathen deities.

In Scotland, there are few references to witchcraft before the Protestant Reformation in the sixteenth century. The trials at North Berwick, in 1597, introduced the idea of a pact with Satan for the first time in Scotland, as a group of witches claimed they had entered into a pact to raise storms for the purpose of destroying James IV.

A POOR EXCUSE

*Some historians have pointed out
a correlation between outbreaks of
witch-hunts and periods of
economic instability. The contrast
between kings, lawyers and
ministers who prided themselves
on their education and learning
and their intellectual rationalism,
while at the same time obsessed
with superstition, perhaps requires
a more complex explanation. The
occasional publicity accorded to
'white witches' in the Highlands
and Islands suggests that our
veneer of rationalism may still be
quite thin.*

Janet Man declared that Janet McNeill had cured her sick child with a charm said in Gaelic, after which she tied a thread around the child's neck, crossed it over his chest, under his arms, and tied it behind his back. After two days she cut the thread off and burned it in the fire – and the child was cured. Somebody thought she might have killed a cat by tying a thread around it, and John Campbell said that he remembered that his cat had died that very day.

Katherine Moore was supposed to have a spell to combat 'ane evill eye' and several people attested that she used her powers to do good, curing animals and people alike. Margrat McLevin also used her powers for good, according to the evidence of John McFersoune. He declared that about three years ago he and some other fishermen were caught in 'a mightie great storm quhich [which] drove them to hazard of the losse of Lyfe and boat'. The storm lasted for three to four hours, then suddenly calmed. They continued with their fishing trip, but on their return Margrat McLevin approached him and said that he should give her something, for he was in her debt: 'I helped you that night quhich [which] if I had not done ye had gone to parteins and become lost' [ie, have become food for crabs!].

This same woman was also accused of placing her 'charme' in tallow or herbs as an ointment and applying it in her healing – John Mctyre the tailor had a sore shoulder which she helped with her ointment. Margrat McLevin spoke openly about her talents and volunteered that she had a good luck charm: 'which is good for preserveing from mischance quhilk she repeited in the yrish language'.

Yet she also confessed before John Glass, the provost of Rothesay, Niniane Ballantyne of Kames, Major David Ramsay and Bailie Walter Stewart that, 'the devill came to her in the lyknes of a man'. She also confessed to meeting 'with severall other witches betwixt Kilmachalmok and Edinmore' and to meeting with other women on several occasions. Some women were seen dancing on the moors, either alone or in small groups. They were blamed for some deaths, of both children and adults.

On 21 February 1662, Issobel McNicoll was apprehended and kept in custody. She was full of remorse, and praying to God for forgiveness and to deliver her soul from the power of Satan. She 'confessed that as she was in her owne house her alone drawing acquavittie, the devil came to her in the lyknes of a young man'. That is, she was in her own house, drinking whisky alone, fantasising about a young man. Not perhaps so difficult to understand.

Several of the women mentioned things they had done, or events which had happened around the time of 'Hallowday' – what we call Hallowe'en. And so it goes on. Margaret McWilliam 'was tried for the merk' – was examined for 'witches marks', three of which were duly found, one on the shin bone of her left leg, another 'betwixt her shoulders' and a third 'up her hensh, blew' (on her 'haunch' and coloured blue). She also confessed that eighteen years before, the devil had appeared to her and had

The Kingarth stone circle

promised to rescue her from poverty and restore her fortunes if she gave him her son William, then seven years old: 'he gave her ane elf errow stone to shott him which she did'. This elfin arrow stone was undoubtedly a prehistoric flint arrowhead, examples of which can be seen in the Bute Museum today. Ten days after following the devil's advice the child died, 'which grieved her most of anything that ever she did'.

Jonet Morisoune was also locked up in the Tolbooth in Rothesay and confessed to covenants with the devil, meetings with other 'witches' and various acts of witchcraft. Sara Stewart declared that she told Jonet that one of her cows was sick, and asked her to take a look at it to see if she could do it any good, and that 'the said Jonet went into the byre and took off her curcheffe [kerchief] and Strek thrie straiks of her curcheffe upon the kow that therafter the kow grew wele'. However, it never again gave milk or calved.

10 WALKS AND EXCURSIONS

BECAUSE BUTE IS SUCH a small island – 15 miles (24km) long by 5 miles (8km) wide at its maximum extent – there are not really any opportunities for long-distance walking, but there are plenty of chances for interesting and diverse half-day excursions. However, walkers who have already knocked off the 95 miles (153km) of the West Highland Way and crossed the Cairngorms through the Lairig Ghru might like to consider adding another, smaller leaf to their laurels – the West Island Way. This is being promoted by the Bute Tourism Management Programme, co-ordinated by Argyll and the Isles Enterprise (the Local Enterprise Company, or LEC), as part of a range of projects which will encourage walkers to come to the island to tackle a 'middle-distance' walk. The route avoids the SSSI (Site of Special Scientific Interest) at the north end of Bute and winds through the south and central parts of the island, through woodland, coasts and moors. It is designed for the mass market – advertised as not needing hiking boots, and marketed as being within easy reach of the urban population of West Central Scotland.

New signposts have been erected, and parts of the route upgraded, to accommodate the expected influx of walkers. For people living on Bute, or spending a holiday there, these initiatives have made it a lot easier to explore the island on foot, without risk of incurring the wrath of farmers or estate managers. A leaflet prepared by Footprint for the tourist board has selected eight walks for promotion.

Ettrick Bay to Kilmichael – 9 miles (14.5km), 4–5 hours. This starts from the car park at Ettrick Bay and explores the archaeology of north-west Bute, from the Neolithic chambered tombs of 2500BC to the early Christian chapel at Kilmichael.

Skipper Wood – 2¹/₂ miles (4km), 1¹/₂ hours. This starts from the centre of Rothesay and wanders through the Bogany Wood, also known as Skipper Wood, on the hillside overlooking the town, returning by way of the golf course to Serpentine Road and the town centre, with a detour to the Canada Hill viewpoint possible.

The inviting isle of Arran, seen from Dunagoil

The Right to Roam

There is plenty of room to roam on Bute, but because the island is farmed very intensively, it is advisable to check with farmers before walking on their land. Scottish walkers guard their rights ferociously, but sometimes it is just a matter of common courtesy to let farmers know your intentions, without necessarily asking for permission – and if there is any problem, it is often possible to accommodate a farmer's concerns.

There are some Sites of Special Scientific Interest (SSSIs) on Bute which are best avoided in order to preserve their ecology. The Tourist Information Centre in Rothesay, Bute Museum and other outlets can supply appropriate maps and leaflets.

The Moor Road – 10 miles (16km), 3–5 hours. Another circular walk starting and finishing in Rothesay, past Loch Ascog and over the Moor Road to the War Memorial on the main road near Mount Stuart. On a clear day this walk gives wide vistas from its moorland vantage points – from the rounded hills of Cowal to the jagged peaks of Arran.

Barone Hill – 3½ miles (5.5km), 2½ hours. A steep and strenuous walk to the prominent viewpoint of Barone Hill, overlooking Rothesay, with the reward of stunning views encompassing most of Bute and the panoramic landscapes beyond.

St Ninian's Bay – 2 miles (3km), 1 hour. An easy walk around the horseshoe of St Ninian's Bay from the village of Straad to the early Christian chapel on St Ninian's Point, taking in two Bronze Age standing stones and a kippering shed, with wonderful views of the Arran mountains.

Glencallum Bay and St Blane's – 4½ miles (7km), 2–4 hours. A varied walk starting at Kilchattan Bay, passing the ruins of Kelspoke Castle and wandering round the southern headlands of Bute to St Blane's chapel, returning to Kilchattan by way of the abandoned township of Kingaven and Suidhe Hill. Again, there are spectacular views in good weather.

The Pioneer *arriving at Rothesay*

Black Park Plantation – 3 miles (5km), 1–2 hours. A walk across the width of the island from Kilchattan Bay to Stravanan Bay from the east coast to the west coast, taking in the remnants of the stone circle in the Black Park plantation and returning to Kilchattan Bay.

Garrison Road, Port Bannatyne – 1 mile (1.5km), 1 hour. An easy walk, sheltered from the prevailing winds and feasible even on a wet day. On a clear day there are good views of the hills of Cowal and the Firth of Clyde.

Of course, these are just some suggestions. Part of the excitement and joy of exploring an island is in finding your own way around, off the beaten track into the many bays and coves, hollows and glades which make Bute so attractive. Rothesay is only ninety minutes from the centre of Glasgow and yet is truly in another world. It is possible to catch the train after work on a Friday at 17.15 and to arrive at Rothesay at 18.45; and then on a Monday morning catch the 07.15 ferry from Rothesay and be in Glasgow by 08.45, leaving two full days of a weekend to explore the island. But why not come and stay for a week, or two, or more, and really get to know the place? And then, as many visitors do, come back next year, and the year after? Whatever time you can spare for Bute, you will be rewarded with a warm welcome and a wonderful island experience.

VISIT THE MAINLAND

Visitors planning to stay on Bute for a week or two might like to consider taking a day to explore the neighbouring mainland district of Cowal, using the Rhubodach to Colintraive ferry. A day-trip to Strachur, Inveraray or Dunoon, returning to Bute in the evening, is eminently possible.

USEFUL INFORMATION AND PLACES TO VISIT

Tourist Information Centre, Rothesay
Isle of Bute Tourist Information Centre, 14 Victoria Street, Rothesay, PA20 0AJ
Tel: 01700 502151; Fax: 01700 505156
Accommodation bookings, leaflets, books, maps. Information on bus services, taxis, services, events, festivals, yacht charters etc. Open all year.

Caledonian MacBrayne, Rothesay
The Ferry Terminal, Rothesay, Isle of Bute, PA20 9AQ
Tel: 01700 502707
Brochure hotline: 01475 650288.

Above: The fountains near the Winter Garden on the Esplanade, Rothesay

Left: The paddle steamer Waverley *at Rothesay*

Paddle Steamer *Waverley*
Waverley Excursions Ltd, Anderston Quay, Glasgow, G3 8HA
Tel: 0141 221 8152
Information on excursions from Bute also available from the Tourist Information Centre in Rothesay.

Local newspaper, *The Buteman*
10 Castle Street, Rothesay, Isle of Bute, PA20 9HB
Tel: 01700 502503/502931
Published weekly on Friday.

PLACES TO VISIT

Ardencraig Gardens and Aviary
6 Ardencraig Lane, Craigmore, Rothesay, Isle of Bute, PA20 9EZ

Tel: 01700 504644
Open May–Sept, 10.00–16.30; Sat–Sun 13.00–16.30.

Ascog Hall Fernery and Gardens
Ascog, Isle of Bute, PA20 9EU
Tel: 01700 504555
Admission charged.

The Bute Museum
Stuart Street, Rothesay, Isle of Bute, PA20 0BX
Tel: 01700 505067
Open Apr–Sept, Mon–Sat 10.30–16.30; Sun14.30–16.30;
Oct–Mar, Tues–Sat 14.30–16.30.

Mount Stuart House and Gardens
Mount Stuart, Isle of Bute, PA20 9LR
Tel: 01700 503877; Fax: 01700 505313
Open May–Sept (with some additional opening times in April and Oct): House 11.00–17.00; gardens 10.00–17.00. **Closed Tues and Thurs.** No dogs allowed in the house or grounds, except for guide dogs. Admission charged.

Rothesay Castle
Rothesay, Isle of Bute
Tel: 01700 502691
Open all year. Apr–Sept, Mon–Sat 09.30–18.30; Sun 14.00–18.30.
Oct–Mar, Mon–Sat 09.30–16.30; Sun 14.00–16.30.
Closed Thurs pm and Fri. Admission charged.

Rothesay Creamery
The Creamery, Rothesay, Isle of Bute, PA20 9JH
Tel: 01700 503186
Open May–Aug 11.00–15.00.

Rothesay Library
Stuart Street, Rothesay, Isle of Bute; PA20 0BX
Tel: 01700 503266; Fax: 01700 500511
Open Tues and Thurs 10.00–13.00, 14.00–19.00;
Wed, Fri and Sat 10.00–13.00, 14.00–17.00. **Closed on Mondays.**

The Winter Garden
Victoria Street, Rothesay, Isle of Bute, PA20 0AH

Tel: 01700 502487; Fax: 01700 505462
Auditorium, cinema, restaurant. Open all year.

THINGS TO DO

Ardbeg Bowling Club
7 Ardbeg Road, Rothesay, Isle of Bute, PA20 0NJ
Tel: 01700 502164
Open May–Sept 10.00–12.00, 14.00–16.00, 19.00–21.30. Admission charged.

Kingarth Trekking Centre
Old School, Kilchattan Bay, Isle of Bute, PA20 9LU
Tel: 01700 831295/831627
Open all year 10.00–16.00.

Loch Fad Fishery
Isle of Bute Trout Co Ltd, Ardmaleish, Isle of Bute, PA20 0QJ
Tel: 01700 504871/502451; Fax: 01700 505127
Open for boats 1 Mar–31 Oct; bank fishing 15 Mar–6 Oct.

Port Bannatyne Golf Club
Bannatyne Main Road, Port Bannatyne, Isle of Bute
Tel: 01700 505073
Admission charged.

Rothesay Bowling Club
Ballochgoy Road, Rothesay, Isle of Bute, PA20 0JE
Tel: 01700 502315
Open all year, daily 14.30–16.30, 18.30–21.00. Admission charged.

Rothesay Golf Course
Canada Hill, Rothesay, Isle of Bute, PA20 9HN
Tel: 01700 503554
Open all year, 08.00 until late daily. Admission charged.

Swimming Pool
Rothesay Leisure Pool, High Street, Rothesay, Isle of Bute, PA20 9BN
Tel: 01700 504300 ext 217
Open weekends until 17.00; weekdays until 21.00.

FURTHER READING

The older books on this list may be difficult to obtain outside of the largest reference libraries, but all are available at the Public Library in Rothesay. Ian Munro's book *The Island of Bute*, from the David & Charles 'Island' series, has an excellent bibliography of books and articles relating to Bute, while Dorothy Marshall's *History of Bute* gives references to articles of archaeological and historical interest. The *Transactions of the Buteshire Natural History Society* contain many interesting and important articles on many aspects of the natural history, archaeology, history and culture of the island.

Blain, John. *History of Bute* (1880)

Buteshire Natural History Society. *Nature Trails*

Downie, R. Angus. *Bute and the Cumbraes* (1934)

Footprint. *The Isle of Bute: a map/guide to eight easy-to-follow walks* (1998)

Hewison, J. King. *The Isle of Bute in the Olden Times* (2 vols; 1893–5)

Marshall, Dorothy N. *History of Bute* (1992)

Munro, Ian S. *The Island of Bute* (David & Charles, 1973)

Pringle, Denys. *Rothesay Castle and St Mary's Church* (Historic Scotland, 1995)

Reid, John Eaton. *History of the County of Bute* (1864)

Stamp, Gavin (ed.). *Mount Stuart House and Gardens* (Mount Stuart Trust, 1995)

Swan, Andrew. *Rothesay and the Stewarts, and Various Visitors* (1990)

Tranter, Nigel. *The Fortified House in Scotland* (1977)

The pier, harbour and town centre of Rothesay

INDEX

Page numbers in *italic* indicate illustrations

Kerrycroy Bay

ACKNOWLEDGEMENTS

Thanks are due to the staff of Rothesay Public Library and The Bute Museum for their friendly welcome and helpfulness; to the staff of the Tourist Information Centre, Rothesay, for much useful advice; to the Mount Stuart Trust for access to the house and gardens in the off season; and to those friends and colleagues who gave their support and recollections of good times on Bute; also to photographer Derek Croucher, for his sympathetic eye and professional skill, and to the staff of David & Charles, the publishers, for their constant support and encouragement, despite the pressure of deadlines.